THE PATH TO RICHES

IN THINK AND GROW RICH

Judith Williamson

AND **Contributing Authors**

T0145547

An Approved Publication of The Napoleon Hill Foundation

MEDIA

MEDIA

Published 2019 by Gildan Media LLC
aka G&D Media
www.GandDmedia.com

Front Cover design by David Rheinhardt of Pyrographx

Interior design by Meghan Day Healey of Story Horse, LLC

Library of Congress Cataloging-in-Publication Data is available upon request

ISBN: 978-1-7225-0110-5

10 9 8 7 6 5 4 3 2 1

CONTENTS

INTRODUCTION

How Ideas Work

by Mitch Horowitz

Every contributor to *The Path to Riches* shares a common bond: their lives have been radically improved by the teachings of Napoleon Hill. Mine has, too. But it took me a while to get there.

For many years, I considered myself a fan of *Think and Grow Rich*. Yet for those same years, I derived relatively little benefit from the book. This is because I dipped into it and skimmed the text, thinking that, as a longtime student of self-development methods, I was already familiar with some of the author's exercises and I had even done them in other contexts. I approached *Think and Grow Rich* with the same divided attention that passengers give to airline safety videos.

I had no idea what I missing.

In 2013, however, I took radically different approach. At that time, I was rethinking my life and career. I decided to get a fresh copy of *Think and Grow Rich* and I committed to reading it and doing all of its steps and exercises *as though my life depended on it.* I threw myself into the book with steely determination. This was the formula that cracked things open. My life and work began to improve in myriad ways.

As I sharped my Definite Chief Aim (a term Hill capitalizes), and worked through the book's principles and exercises as if I were studying for med school finals, I experienced new and deepened opportunities as a writer, speaker, TV host, and narrator. My remuneration increased dramatically. I often view my life today as divided in two halves: before and after my dedicated study of *Think and Grow Rich.*

As the contributors to *The Path to Riches* explore, there is nothing superfluous, extra, or unnecessary in *Think and Grow Rich*, or in any of Hill's books. Each and every step is vital and intimately connected to all of the others. There is no halfway approach to his program. For that very reason, *The Path to Riches* is of great value to the student of self-development. Its engaging and short chapters highlight Hill's rules and ideas in ways that refresh them in your mind, and keep you working with Hill's *full program.*

In some ways our society has grown too "sophisticated." Or, put differently, too cynical. We think that because we've already heard of a certain principle, or because an ethic or idea may seem familiar, we "get it." But we do not get it. That is an illusion. If simple ethical ideas were as understandable and actionable as we think, we'd all be living by the Golden Rule. There would be no addiction, gossip, or senseless violence. But we, as a human community, are made up of hearers and not doers of the word. This is one of the core maladies of human nature. It is among the reasons why valuable ideas of wisdom and self-help, like Hill's, go unheeded.

Reminding yourself of, and rededicating yourself to, life-giving ideas is *always* a worthy pursuit. It always pays off. *The*

Path to Riches gives you that very opportunity with the ideas of Napoleon Hill. Run and embrace it.

Mitch Horowitz the PEN Award-winning author of books including *Occult America* and *The Miracle Club: How Thoughts Become Reality.* Visit him @MitchHorowitz.

Somewhere, as you read, the secret to which I refer will jump from the page and stand boldly before you, if you are ready for it! When it appears, you will recognize it. Whether you receive the sign in the first or the last chapter, stop for a moment when it presents itself, and turn down a glass, for that occasion will mark the most important turning-point of your life.

—NAPOLEON HILL

Foreword

The Magic IS Inside YOU!

by Judith Williamson
VALPARAISO, INDIANA

Think and Grow Rich is the bestselling, all time motivational classic that continues to daily inspire countless people of all nations and nationalities in all walks of life. This book is without a shelf-life and grabs the reader's attention from the very first sentence—

> Truly, "thoughts are things," and powerful things at that, when they are mixed with definiteness of purpose, persistence, and a burning desire for their translation into riches, or other material objects.

Its mesmerizing hold on every type of reader attests to the deep seated awareness in personal motivation that the author Napoleon Hill had as he penned this book. Dr. Hill's desire to share the formula for the acquisition of riches lasted his entire lifetime. He read, interviewed, collected, and fine-tuned his research until he was able to offer the world the riches that this single volume book shares. The treasure in *Think and Grow*

Rich is vast and not the same for each reader. Whether a person is seeking financial, spiritual, physical, or emotional richness depends upon where they are in life's journey. Understanding this journey of life is one of the multiple keys to unlocking the door and receiving the secret that Napoleon Hill states stands directly before you as you read his book. Still, the question remains, "How does one go about harnessing the riches that are so openly discussed in this 1937 classic?"

I am not the first to tell you that many readers fail to uncover the "secret" contained between the pages of the book. People read and reread the book countless times and still come up missing the key that Dr. Hill has so very openly revealed in his writing. Some people look for a hidden code, for an offbeat idea or something even related to the occult, but let me assure you, stop looking for fool's gold because the secret is none of these.

Consistently, I receive inquiries regarding where the secret lies buried in the book, how to locate the promised secret, and then how to put it to immediate income producing use. People have even accused the Foundation of selfishly refusing to reveal the exact secret for fear of financial loss. All of these seekers are failing to see how the secret is right where it always was—inside each of them. When confronted with this possibility, individuals fail to believe the likelihood of this profound treasure being inside themselves—placed at birth by a benevolent Creator who made it each individual's challenge in life to develop his or her potential to the fullest.

I know many successful individuals who have found the secret by reading this book and who have applied it to their personal benefit in life. I also know many people who have read the book several times and are no better off than before they read it. What makes the difference in the effect that the book produces, and how does a person go about acquiring the ability to mine the riches buried in this inspiring self-help classic?

First, consider the idea that success in life is generally triggered by some sort of action performed by a person. This success producing action also relates to an area of intense personal interest that the doer has discovered in himself. This person knows what he likes and what he doesn't like. What he is good at doing, and not so good at doing. In short, he has conducted a personal self-analysis and has a good idea of who he is.

Second, thought alone is insufficient for the production of results. Thought plus action is the repeatable formula that generates results in a person's life. Thought is the forerunner of action, and the truth is successful people follow thought with immediate action to create positive outcomes in their lives.

Third, thought that is emotionalized will produce quicker results when translated into action because the heart and mind have been engaged in the total process and raise the level of energy directed toward the outcome. Motives, both positive and negative, contribute to an accelerated process of goal achievement. Make sure that your desire is not a neutral or a cool desire, but has the white heat of emotionalized intensity if you want to see results soon. My self-proclaimed formula for success that I share with my students is: Thought + Emotionalized Action = Success. I always work under the assumption that the goal in question is a positive one in order for the outcome to be positive as well.

But, you don't have to take my word for it. In recognition of those individuals who have unlocked the secret in *Think and Grow Rich*, I have requested that they share some treasure hunting tips with Dr. Hill's readers. All have agreed to offer their findings. In this book entitled *Path to Riches*, twenty-three readers of *Think and Grow Rich* offer you a chance to learn from their journey.

Napoleon Hill often reminds us that when the student is ready the teacher will appear. This book offers you, the student, an extravaganza of teachers, guides for your journey, perhaps soul mates, who are certain that they have uncovered and applied the secret in *Think and Grow Rich* in their lives. Not only that, but they have greatly improved their lives due to their reading and application of this profound book.

In concluding his book, Napoleon Hill quotes Emerson as he states: "If we are related, we have, through these pages, met." Likewise, if you are a sincere seeker of the secret that Dr. Hill promises to deliver in his book, you will find the people in *Path to Riches* as family who will guide you in the direction of your search. Each contributor has given freely without compensation of their time and talent to aid you in your search for the truth. Each has gone the extra mile to contribute the "secret" that they uncovered in the hope that it will serve as a signpost for you as you travel towards life's riches.

May you have a special relationship with our contributors and remember to thank the ones in particular who helped you uncover the secret to your success!

Be Your Very Best Always,
Judith Williamson

About Judith Williamson

Judith Williamson, Director of the Napoleon Hill World Learning Center at Purdue University Calumet, has been studying Napoleon Hill's motivational philosophy for over 25 years. She has taught Dr. Hill's

Science of Success to students around the world and authored several books in collaboration with the Foundation. A former public school teacher and administrator, Judy's passion for education drives the Foundation's successful outreach projects and leadership programs.

1

"Oh, Lord, won't you buy me a Mercedes Benz?"

—Janis Joplin

by Dr. J.B. Hill
BRIDGEPORT, WEST VIRGINIA

Let me state up front that my bloodline does not give me any special knowledge or insight into my grandfather Napoleon Hill or his philosophy of success. At best, my relationship allowed me to make use of his philosophy earlier in my life than others have but I remain his student to this day. I am awed by what he wrote.

Many, many people have read and even studied *Think and Grow Rich* but never seem to put it together. Why not? Is there really a secret hidden within? Or is it a case of the Emperor's New Clothes? The answer is yes, there is indeed a secret and it hides behind its own simplicity. In spite of this, Napoleon Hill declined to spell it out, allegedly because the secret works "best" for those who uncover it for themselves.

Napoleon Hill used 381 pages of typed text to outline the secret; however, it came to me as just four one-syllable words.

Unfortunately, I do not think that I can convey full understanding so succinctly. A tangential presentation may be necessary and this may be the reason why Hill crafted it into book form. I don't know; I do know, that I also find myself forced to provide context to add meaning. Try describing the richness that color brings to life to a person who is color blind. It can be done but full understanding can only be achieved by conceptualizing through analogy.

If Hill was correct about self-discovery, making the secret more esoteric may not be in the best interest of those likely to read this. However, I know from personal experience that it cannot be fully grasped until the time is right and that its understanding is very personal. When it came to me, the hair stood up on the back of my neck before calmness beset me. It was personal, very personal—as personal as salvation. There is a universal truth to salvation that we can easily discern but complete understanding only comes with *personal* salvation. It has to be experienced. We choose to believe, we choose to be saved. We choose to succeed.

So, I am going to tell you what I discovered so long ago that changed my life forever. I suppose it all started when I was 12 years old and I was introduced to my grandfather. We spent two days with him in Greenville, S.C. While I was there, Napoleon gave me a copy of *Think and Grow Rich* signed in green ink on the inside cover. He put the book into my hands and told me to read it. I promised him that I would.

I read the book that summer, and while I thought it was entertaining, it certainly did not light a fire in me. At 12, I really had no goals except to stay out of trouble. I just wasn't ready for the book. This changed.

By the time I was 23, I had begun to realize that I was on a path that just wasn't right for me. I had asserted independence early from my family and had been making my own decisions for some time. Unfortunately, I was also living with the results of my decision making. I lost a full scholarship, quit college, and was drafted into the armed forces as a private. I was alone, lonely, and had started to drift through life.

Drifting is one of the greatest reasons for failure in life. It is done by people who cannot or will not make the decision to take action. It is done by those who have lost the focus needed to sustain the drive towards their goals. It is done by those trapped in their job by its security and comfort. And it is done by everyone without a goal.

I fell into that last group . . . those without a goal. I was drifting through life—waiting for something to happen. I knew that I needed to make a change in my life . . . but how? I had no money, no education, and could not bring myself to ask my family for help.

The answer came to me after I bought another copy of *Think and Grow Rich* and took it home to read. This time I was more receptive and read the book through twice. My first reading left me excited but revealed no secret. I knew I had missed something so I started a second read, taking notes. I had reached the section on excuses near the end of the book when the hair started to stand up on the back of my neck and I began to understand. I remember writing that if I wanted to make this work, I had to accept it on faith and commit myself to it.

I decided to return to school and made a plan that I put into action. It worked. One year later, I found myself at Vanderbilt University studying engineering. Three and a half years later, I graduated 12th in my class from one of the finest schools in America. I was transformed.

To get there, I applied the steps that I had read about in *Think and Grow Rich*. I picked a goal, went the extra mile, used the subconscious mind, . . . I did it all and managed to make my way to college on full scholarship, finish early, and graduate with honors. So, I achieved success by using the principles that my grandfather told us to use. But that was not and is not the secret given in *Think and Grow Rich*. It was just the recipe for success and hardly made the hair stand up on the back of my neck. Something else did.

General George Goethals[1] once admonished his subordinates; "When do you expect to do the wonderful things you are dreaming about? Why don't you begin? What are you waiting for? Where is your courage? Why don't you start? Are you waiting for a good thing to come to you, waiting for influence, for pull, for someone to help you? If you have formed the habit of putting off, of deliberating, waiting for better conditions, you will never get anywhere in the world. The first thing is to begin. The world is full of people who are either failures or who are plodding along in mediocrity because they didn't care to begin, to launch out. *'Didn't dare to begin'* would make a fitting epitaph for millions of nobodies, millions of failures."[2]

Elbert Hubbard[3] wrote: "The world bestows its big prizes, both in money and honors, for but one thing. And that is initiative."

So, initiative and taking action are clearly important. Hill, Goethals and Hubbard certainly thought so and B.C. Forbes and Clement Stone as well. Yes, I took the initiative to change my life and I took the action that I needed to achieve success but, again, that was not and is not the secret given to me in

---

1 Major Gen. George Washington Goethals was known as the builder of the Panama Canal and served as the first Civil Governor of the Panama Canal Zone.

2 *Keys to Success* by B.C. Forbes; Page 102; Copyright, 1917, 1918, 1926.

3 Elbert Green Hubbard (June 19, 1856–May 7, 1915) was an America writer, publisher, artist, and philosopher who wrote *A Message to Garcia*.

Think and Grow Rich. It was just part of the recipe that we all know so well. Something else did.

When I read *Think and Grow Rich* for the second time so long ago, I realized that I held the recipe for success in my hands. It was the key to everything—financial security, personal relationships, happiness . . . it could be used to achieve anything of value. It could be done by anybody and it could be done by me. There was just one catch. It's up to me.[1]

About Dr. J.B. Hill

Dr. J.B. Hill is the son of David Hill, the youngest son of Napoleon Hill. Dr. Hill is a retired Marine and holds degrees in engineering, mathematics, and medicine. He is board certified in family medicine and practices in Bridgeport, WV. Dr. Hill can be reached through the Napoleon Hill World Learning Center, 2300 173rd Street; Hammond, IN 46323-2094.

---

1 *"All great truths are simple in final analysis, and easily understood; if they are not, they are not great truths."*—Napoleon Hill

2

The Secret to Napoleon Hill's Think and Grow Rich

by Philip McCauley
DUBLIN, IRELAND

The Students await . . . the Master

It is said that "when the student is ready . . . the Master will appear!" While on the face of it this may be a universally accepted principle . . . the rule does not strictly apply in my chosen profession. I am lucky enough to have the opportunity each and every day to encounter many, many students . . . who are not necessarily ready or willing to encounter a Master . . . any Master . . . and therein lies the secret to their success!

"Educo" the word meaning to "draw out, to educe or to develop from within" is the correct ideology which should apply to the field of education. Sadly however, it is the opposite which is more often applied. In my role as a secondary or high school teacher, I witness daily, a system of education which is applied and enforced throughout the western world and beyond. It is a system which I firmly believe flies in the face of all that can and should be developed and nurtured in the field of education. The system to which I refer is one which assumes that all students should be treated merely as "empty vessels" waiting to be filled. It is a system which kills the spirit, quenches the thirst for "specialized knowledge" and oftentimes . . . destroys the souls of many a mere mortal. The general system of educating our students which exists today should be put on trial, scrutinized and asked to account for herself while facing the charge of truly failing to educate her students. I for one already know the verdict . . . guilty as charged. As a witness for the prosecution I would call upon the testimony of some of the most educated and successful people in the world and Henry Ford, John Wanamaker and Thomas Edison spring to mind. Educated, YES . . . schooled, NO!

As someone who has been on the frontline of education for more than twelve years, I can safely say that I experienced at first hand, an intense level of frustration that I shared with both my students and colleagues alike. This was a frustration born of being bound by the shackles of conformity and endless syllabi. This frustration is one which is shared by many people in the field of frontline education. The blatant lack of "financial education" and the failure to promote "free thinking" in our schools is indicative of a system that stifles the very essence and free spirit of education and is one which creates employees rather than employers, followers rather than successful leaders! My frustration with this system was dissolved the moment I discovered the "secret" that lay silently awaiting its discovery between the dusty covers of a well leafed copy of Dr. Napoleon Hill's *Think and Grow Rich!*

Think and Grow Rich is a book which calls to you from the bookshelf. Its very title draws you in like a mermaid drawing fishermen onto the rocks! Once you commit to reading it . . . it has a narcotic style and substance. Any book which commits to its reader, the promise of the secret of abundant wealth has got to be worth the cover price if nothing else. I was intrigued and I decided to commit to uncovering the "secret" which the author promises in his preface is mentioned no fewer than one hundred times throughout the course of the book. What grabbed my attention was the fact that Dr. Hill promises only to "mention" the secret rather than explicitly state the secret! He tells us that the secret is in fact laid bare before the readers eyes, and yet so many people report to having failed to see it. How can this be? How can a secret be put into print no fewer than one hundred times in one book and yet people fail to identify it? This was a journey of discovery that I set out upon alone and now thankfully, I have brought the road map to the attention of many of my students and I have dared them to take "the road less travelled." It was along this very road that I uncovered the secret to *Think and Grow Rich.*

Tools of the trade

As an educator, books tend to be the tools of my craft and generally they prescribe a set course to follow, which if followed correctly will lead you to a desired destination. Not so in the book *Think and Grow Rich.* Here is a book which suggests that one may uncover its "reason d'être" in the first or last chapter and indeed in any chapter in between. What kind of book I thought can be written which is capable of fulfilling its very purpose in chapter one . . . but only if you can see it! This premise flies in the face of the system of education to which many attribute some of their success. A system in which one must follow a prescribed set of rules to reach a set destination!

Yet 500 of the world's wealthiest people attribute THEIR success, to having uncovered this alternative route and secret to success, albeit in chapter one or indeed the last chapter of *Think and Grow Rich!*

Where and what is the secret?

So how can one begin to search for a secret if you don't in fact know what exactly it is that you are looking for? And having uncovered it how can one be sure that it really is the secret? After all, isn't a secret supposed to be just that . . . a secret! Something purposely hidden away from those who are not supposed to be in the "know" so to speak. By its very nature, a secret is not supposed to be shared, discussed or passed on, but to a chosen few. Therein lies the genius of Dr. Napoleon Hill. Having being given the secret "when Andrew Carnegie . . . the canny, loveable Scotsman carelessly tossed it into his mind when he was but a boy" he was permitted and indeed instructed to pass it on and make it publically available, but ONLY to those who would make full use of its power, not abuse the possibilities it holds and to ensure that it would not be lost for future generations to come. So the challenge that was laid before Napoleon Hill was, to spend twenty years accumulating the knowledge and wisdom to create a road map to the treasured secret. Then he was to make the map available to all, but only possible to be read by those "willing and determined enough" to stay the course, follow the path, seek directions, read the signposts and ensure that when they arrived at their destination they would know beyond doubt that "yes, I have arrived"! Indeed Napoleon Hill instructs the reader in his preface that "when it appears, you will recognize it.

Whether you receive the sign in the first or last chapter, stop for a moment when it presents itself and raise your glass to toast your epiphany."

I explain to my students that this is how and why the book came into existence and why millions of copies have been sold worldwide. This, I explain is why more people throughout history attribute their success to having read THIS book than any other book ever printed! I then proceed to set out the task before my students in school to pick up the map, set out upon the road, and seek to uncover the Carnegie secret to abundant wealth. It is at this very moment that I actually witness the secret in action first hand!

The Secret in Action

In my opening paragraph I alluded to the fact that some students are not always very receptive to the idea of being formally tutored or instructed! It is in this resistance that I discovered the Carnegie secret.

I have been privileged to teach students for thirteen years in what has been designated as a disadvantaged school. This designation assumes that the students are from many diverse and socially disadvantaged backgrounds, including broken homes, single parent families and various levels of poverty.

I say privileged because it has been through my daily interaction with my students that I have come to uncover the Carnegie secret. The secret in *Think and Grow Rich* is indeed a simple one but when called upon and put into action it has a formidable force which knows no bounds, recognizes no limits or borders and can tear down ANY obstacle that may be foolish enough to attempt to obstruct it! The secret to which I refer is one which I believe is best discovered through the mindset and eyes of a child . . . because, when viewed through this prism it is at its most potent!

Disadvantaged students tend to come from such a variety of backgrounds and ideologies that it would be unwise and indeed unfair to attempt to draw comparisons. However, throughout my years of teaching, I have come to identify a very clear and distinct common trait which bonds my students together and sets them apart from others I know and it is this; an absolute unwavering determination to resist the system which binds them and a sense of loyalty that no money could ever buy! Having read *Think and Grow Rich*, I wondered what might happen if I presented some of these students with the Carnegie roadmap if and when they were ready. I had planned to observe what might gradually evolve from their reading of the book. My preconception of something gradually evolving from my students was my first lesson in the Carnegie secret. It doesn't evolve . . . it literally explodes into existence. So here is HOW I discovered the secret through the eyes and minds of my students!

The Secret Revealed

If I have come to learn anything about the art of teaching it is this. One must decide how relevant the material being taught is to the life of the student TODAY and hone the material accordingly. My students continue to question the relevance of anything being taught in the context of "how will this benefit me directly"? Very few of my students will attend third level schooling and so the importance of very high grades in final exams is not a priority for them. What is a priority for them is their ability to survive independently in an increasingly competitive post education environment and they have an absolute determination and resilience to acquire the knowledge to do so (Desire).

I am teaching in a world where students have 24/7 access to all forms of information they may require in the palm of their hands through the medium of their internet enabled mobile/cell phones. It was in acknowledging this reality that I realized the subtle but life changing difference between information and applied knowledge! My students use applied knowledge to operate on a quasi pain/pleasure principle that I have only become aware of over time. They actively seek enjoyable, pleasurable experiences and avoid anything which may attract pain into their lives. Clearly formal schooling doesn't rank too high on their pleasure graph! They have an innate ability to absorb any information that they need in order to develop their social skills and surround themselves with like-minded students (The Mastermind Principle). They have also established a very loyal network of friends who constantly update and share any information they need to progress in their endeavors (Specialized Knowledge). So it was against this background that I explained to my students about a very interesting book I had come across and how it held within it the secret to abundant wealth!

From a standing start, I watched my students clamour to borrow this book from me and then I saw it develop rapidly into a burning DESIRE to acquire and most importantly APPLY with absolute FAITH the specialized KNOWL-EDGE held within *Think and Grow Rich.*

There is the secret to *Think and Grow Rich!* My students are not bound by any limitations of their mind other than those they may choose to put there themselves. Because they are young enough and skeptical enough of a world that attempts to bind them . . . they have actively resisted the conformist conditioning of a cynical world that most adults have long since succumbed to! My student's minds are like the pages of an empty book. A book in which they and they alone will author their life stories.

My students did not once question the veracity of the book. I did not force it upon them. Rather, I left it along the road they are travelling and offered it as an alternative roadmap to their destinations. People by their very nature are much more open and receptive to acquiring new skills and learning something new if they feel that they themselves have chosen to learn it. In the case of *Think and Grow Rich*, my students devoured the book and could find no difficulty uncovering the secret. They do admit to finding some of the repetitive instructions off putting. This however should be understood against a background of hyperactivity and a low threshold for all things repetitive! My students just "got it" right off the bat! When asked what it is that they got, they will explain the secret in very clear concise language and it is this! The secret to abundant wealth is, an absolute open mind and burning Desire! A mind which is completely untainted by ANY prejudice, bindings or prohibitive thoughts. They understand clearly the damage that a single negative thought can have on ANY plans you have in your imagination (The Workshop Of The Mind). Those who got the "secret" explain it as simply being open to the possibility that EVERYTHING is possible if you only desire it bad enough and if you have a definite plan to attain it. They stress that the most important part is to BEGIN. . . . take ACTION . . . set out along the road immediately and never ever give up until you have reached your destination. If you do give up, it will only be because you did not desire the thing you wanted to achieve. . . . you merely wished for it. Wishes are two a penny and they do not have the faith, desire or commitment to become realities. Hence the world is full of wishes and dreams and short on realities!

So if you want to uncover the secret in *Think and Grow Rich*, here's how. Start the book again from the very beginning. Read it, as if through the eyes of an untainted impressionable teenager. Accept from the very outset that EVERYTHING you read is absolute fact, knowing that a fact is an undisputable statement of truth. A fact which can and has been backed up by countless stories of success. Believe that everything you desire is attainable but only if you follow the book to the letter. Accept two absolute inalienable truths. They are, that you will NOT succeed if you do not have a Definite plan to follow and an absolute unquenchable thirst and Desire to attain your goal. If you do this, you simply cannot fail! Too many people, my own students included have proven this to be true. Know this also. If you the student are not ready for the secret . . . then the Master WILL NOT appear! My students were ready and continue to stand ready to grasp any opportunity which may pass along their paths of life. They quickly identify the opportunity in every adversity. They operate in a twilight world where every single encounter is viewed through the prism of "good luck, bad luck, who knows!" They firmly believe that all things happen for a reason and if you can't see the reason, it's simply that you aren't looking hard enough to find the lesson that life is trying to teach you!

The Master has appeared! He has just instructed you how to find and use the secret in Napoleon Hill's *Think and Grow Rich*. If you still cannot understand how . . . then don't be disheartened. Accept that you the student are not yet ready! Take heart in knowing that half the trick to uncovering the secret is in being out along the roadway with the map in your hand actively looking for it!

I can make you one promise and it is this. If you desperately desire to find the secret to abundant wealth, then you are absolutely guaranteed to find it. The answer is in the roadmap. Begin today along the path less travelled and know you are not a lonely pilgrim. If you happen upon some of my students, tag along for they surely know the way!

About Philip McCauley

Philip McCauley is a young teacher who has been teaching in a secondary school for disadvantaged boys for the past 13 years. The school is in north Dublin, the Capital of the Republic of Ireland.

3

The Hidden Treasure that is in Think and Grow Rich

by Rich Winograd

FORT LAUDERDALE, FLORIDA

What is the secret that is in *Think and Grow Rich* and how can we, the reader, unearth it? I answer this simple question by realizing that one, there is no secret and two, the very first word of the book is the only mechanism that any of us will ever need to unearth all of our potential for personal growth and achievement.

There is no secret. We just need to *think*. And it is our thoughts which become the things we desire.

The notion that the messages, principles and wisdom offered in *Think and Grow Rich* are a secret is an interesting one. It was made more interesting when a book of that very name was published more than fifty years after *Think and Grow Rich* was published, a book which basically repeated the same messages, principles and wisdom that Dr. Hill had already written about. And it was all placed under the umbrella of some phenomenal *secret* just now revealed.

There is no secret. We just need to *think*. And it is our thoughts which become the things we desire.

Now it is worth noting that the concept of a *secret* does appear in *Think and Grow Rich*. Why this was done I cannot say for sure. Dr. Hill certainly had his methods and his reasons. But as the formulas for personal growth and achievement are delivered it became clear to this reader that the use of the word *secret* was unnecessary and inappropriate.

Dr. Hill's own words, from "A Word from the Author:"

In every chapter of this book, mention has been made of the money-making secret which has made fortunes for hundreds of exceedingly wealthy men whom I have carefully analyzed over a long period of years.

The secret was brought to my attention by Andrew Carnegie, more than half a century ago.

This book contains the secret, after having been put to a practical test by thousands of people, in almost every walk of life.

The secret was passed on to thousands of men and women who have used it for their personal benefit, as Mr. Carnegie planned that they should.

The secret to which I refer has been mentioned no fewer than a hundred times throughout this book.

If you are ready to put it to use, you will recognize this secret at least once in every chapter.

The secret to which I refer cannot be had without a price, although the price is far less than its value.

The secret serves equally well all who are ready for it.

Napoleon Hill never once claimed his findings to be his own. Never once did he claim to provide great revelations. Never once did he claim to have a *secret* to give the world. On the contrary, he gave repeated credit to Andrew Carnegie and the many other successful men of his era and stated plainly that his work was his research and his role was simply as messenger.

These were proven methods, thus, not *secrets*. There is then a better word to describe what we unearth in Dr. Hill's work and what leads us to the mechanism for making use of it.

I prefer to call it a hidden treasure.

Have you ever noticed that the word *treasure* is typically preceded by the word *hidden?* The addition of the adjective provides considerable enhancements. First, it conjures up a sense of mystery and intrigue about it. Second, it lends the idea of a journey, a quest, an adventure to obtain it. Third, it establishes a higher value and a sense of importance to it. And finally, it implies the notion of effort, of work, that needs to be put forth for its attainment.

Treasures don't land on one's doorstep. They don't fall from the sky. They're not waiting at the corner of your street. Treasures are hidden. You have to go find them. You have to unearth them. Napoleon Hill's *Think and Grow Rich* is by all accounts a treasure in the field of personal growth and achievement. The profound messages, principles and wisdom which Dr. Hill has placed within the treasure are indeed hidden. This is by masterful design, for the four reasons stated above. It is up to us, the reader, to seek and find them, and by doing so we start the process of *thinking and growing rich.*

Says Dr. Hill of these treasures, "It has not been directly named, for it seems to work more successfully when it is merely uncovered and left in sight, where those who are ready, and searching for it, may pick it up."

Nothing worth having comes easily. There is no free lunch. There is no silver platter. Growth and success take effort and time. We live in an age where we expect ease and simplicity. The great majority, especially today's youth, lack the discipline to understand the value of effort and time. We want it all, we want it now and we want it easily. And when we don't get it all, now and easily, we allow negative qualities such as fear, frustration, procrastination, depression and failure to consume us and define our lives.

The answer is the hidden treasure within the pages of *Think and Grow Rich.*

It starts on page 1. Thoughts Are Things. From the very first example of Edwin C. Barnes, we learn that "thoughts are things, and powerful things at that, when they are mixed with definiteness of purpose, persistence, and a burning desire for their translation into riches, or other material objects."

That's it. That's the message, or the *secret,* if you really insist on using that word. If you never read another page of *Think and Grow Rich* or never read another book written by Napoleon Hill or any other of the countless, excellent books that have been written on personal growth and achievement you have the mechanism to be successful. *Thoughts become things and those thoughts must be backed by a definite major purpose and fueled by persistence and a burning desire for achievement.*

This is what the majority lack. Most people just don't think. Most people have no definite purpose. Most people have no goals. Most people go through life like lost ships at sea and we all know where a ship with no guidance ends up.

Worse yet, many people do think but their thoughts are negative. We learn that laws of nature will ensure that negative thoughts will bring negative results. Fearful thoughts will produce more fear. Thoughts of failure will in turn bring failure.

And for those who have a definite purpose or have specific goals, but lack persistence and a burning desire for achievement, the same troubles will surface. This is where we find quitters, who become failures, who become negative influences.

The answer is quite simple (and not a *secret*). *Think and Grow Rich*. We can now see that this is not merely the title of a book, but rather the most profound formula for success.

We can certainly find the formula repeated beyond page 1. On page 3, Dr. Hill shares the story of "Three Feet from Gold" which serves to show "one of the most common causes of failure, the habit of quitting when one is overtaken by *temporary defeat*." From this story, and countless others similar to it, Dr. Hill would go on to develop one of the most profound of his principles—Learning from Adversity and Defeat. "Every adversity carries with it the seed of an equivalent or greater benefit." Does this tie into something else we've already unearthed? How can a temporary defeat be overcome?

Thoughts become things and those thoughts must be backed by a definite major purpose and fueled by persistence and a burning desire for achievement. Page 1—that's how!

Everything that unfolds in *Think and Grow Rich* can be traced back to this fundamental idea and formula for personal growth and achievement. Dr. Hill also sums it up this way: "Whatever the mind of man can conceive and believe it can achieve."

In 1952, fourteen years after he wrote *Think and Grow Rich*, Napoleon Hill met W. Clement Stone at a dental convention that Hill had been invited to speak at. Out of that meeting, Hill and Stone formed a "Mastermind Alliance" which in turn led to the development of, among other things, a course entitled "PMA (Positive Mental Attitude)—The Science of Success." In the course, 17 core Principles of Success were listed.

These 17 Principles are yet another, great hidden treasure. The purpose of mentioning them here, and listing them below, is to show how these principles are derived from the very simple but profound message delivered on page 1 of *Think and Grow Rich*. Read each principle carefully and see the connection to "thoughts are things, and powerful things at that, when they are mixed with definiteness of purpose, persistence, and a burning desire for their translation into riches, or other material objects."

Definiteness of Purpose

Definiteness of Purpose is the starting point of all achievement and it begins with the adoption of a definite major purpose and a specific plan for its attainment. Without a purpose and a plan, people drift aimlessly throughout life.

Mastermind Alliance

This principle consists of an alliance of two or more minds working together in perfect harmony for the attainment of a definite objective. Success does not come without the cooperation of others.

Applied Faith

Faith is an active state of mind. This belief in yourself is applied to achieving a definite major purpose in life. Faith is an abstract idea, a purely mental concept. Act on it. Action is the first requirement of all faith.

Going the Extra Mile

This is the action of rendering more and better service than that for which you are presently paid. The person who gets ahead does the thing that should be done without being told to do it, but he/she does not stop there. He/She does a great deal more than is expected or demanded of.

Pleasing Personality

Personality is the sum total of one's mental, spiritual, and physical traits and habits that distinguish one from all others. It is the factor that determines whether one is liked or disliked by others. Your personality is your greatest asset or liability.

Personal Initiative

This is the power that inspires the completion of that which one begins. It is the power that starts all action. No person is free until he learns to do his own thinking and gains courage to act on his own.

Positive Mental Attitude

Positive Mental Attitude is the right mental attitude in all circumstances. Keep your mind on the things you want and off the things you don't want. Success attracts more success while failure attracts more failure.

Enthusiasm

Enthusiasm is faith in action. It is the intense emotion known as burning desire. The flame of enthusiasm burning within you turns thought into action.

Self-Discipline

Self-Discipline means taking possession of your own mind. It begins with the mastery of thought. It is the bottleneck through which all of your personal power for success must flow. Direct your thoughts, control your emotions, and ordain your destiny.

Accurate Thinking

The accurate thinker always submits his emotional desires and decisions to his/her head for judiciary examination before he relies upon them as being sound, for he/she knows that the head is more dependable than the heart. The accurate thinker separates facts from fiction and separates facts into two classes: important and unimportant.

Controlled Attention

Controlled attention leads to mastery in any type of human endeavor, because it enables one to focus the powers of his mind upon the attainment of a definite objective and to keep it so directed at will. Great achievements come from minds that are at peace with themselves.

Teamwork

Teamwork is harmonious cooperation that is willing, voluntary and free. Whenever the spirit of teamwork is the dominating influence, success is inevitable. Harmonious cooperation is a priceless asset that you can acquire in proportion to your giving.

Learning from Adversity and Defeat

Every adversity carries with it the seed of an equivalent or greater benefit. Individual success usually is in exact proportion to the scope of the defeat the individual has experienced and mastered. Most so-called failures represent only a temporary defeat that may prove to be a blessing in disguise.

Creative Vision

Creative Vision is developed by the free and fearless use of one's imagination. Creative Vision attains its ends by basically new ideas and methods.

Maintenance of Sound Health

The mind and body are so closely related that whatever one does affects the other. One does not enjoy sound health without a health consciousness. To maintain a health consciousness, one must think in terms of sound health, not in terms of illness and disease.

Budgeting Time and Money

Successful people ask themselves how they are using their time, how much of it is wasted, how is it wasted and what are they doing to stop the waste. Tell me how you use your spare time and how you spend your money and I will tell you where and what you will be ten years from now.

Cosmic Habitforce

Cosmic Habitforce pertains to the universe as a whole and the laws that govern it. It is a sense of order. You are where you are and what you are because of your established habits and thoughts and deeds.

And there's the hidden treasure.

About Rich Winograd

Rich Winograd is a sales executive for a large U.S. corporation. He is also a freelance writer and author of the book *Paloma*, published in 2008 by the Napoleon Hill Foundation. He completed the Napoleon Hill World Learning Center's PMA Science of Success course in 2009 and applies the 17 Principles of Success in every aspect of his life. You can reach him at richwinograd@yahoo.com.

4

Napoleon Hill's famous Secret to Success in All Aspects of Life

by Ray Stendall

SUNNYVALE, CALIFORNIA

Dr. Napoleon Hill dedicated his work to understanding what it takes to be truly successful in all aspects of life. He shared his secret in many of his books and lectures. However, as any teacher, he very much wanted his students to uncover the secret for themselves, as he knew it would mean substantially more to them if they figured it out on their own.

After more than 20 years of studying Napoleon Hill and his personal achievement philosophy, I believe I have uncovered the secret to successful living. Before I divulge the secret, let me remind you of the clues Napoleon Hill openly gave us:

In *Think and Grow Rich,* in the author's preface, he clearly states *"You should have the answer before you finish this book. You may find it in the very first chapter or on the very last page."* Let's examine these two clues: Chapter one is entitled Desire—the starting point of all achievement. In this chapter, Dr. Hill explains the importance of cultivating and having a definite burning desire. Let's now look at the last page of the book. The last page is actually in the epilogue, and he states:

> *"The Master Key is intangible, it is powerful! It is the privilege of creating, in your own mind, a BURNING DESIRE for a definite form of riches. There is no penalty for the use of the key, but there is a price you must pay if you do not use it. The price is FAILURE. There is a reward of stupendous proportion if you put the key to use. It is the satisfaction that comes to all who conquer self and force life to pay whatever is asked."*

Having a deep burning desire to advance is the secret—think of it as an engine that drives you toward success. The secret, however, can be used for either good or evil. Since the purpose of Napoleon Hill's book is to communicate how we can live happy and productive lives, we have to combine this secret with the concept of a "Positive Mental Attitude." A Positive Mental Attitude is the vehicle that helps you attract the people, things and circumstances needed for progress throughout your life as a permanent companion. It is interesting to note that the Positive Mental Attitude concept was central to his work in the *Law of Success* series. That series was written well before *Think and Grow Rich*. This concept also served as the title of the certification program for all future students/teachers of Napoleon Hill's philosophy.

The rest of this chapter will showcase additional evidence that supports the secret of a DEFINITE BURNING DESIRE with a POSITIVE MENTAL ATTITUDE.

Definiteness of Purpose and Burning Desire

As discussed above, Dr. Hill openly tells us the secret in chapter one—cultivate and maintain a burning desire.

This burning desire needs to be written down in a "Definiteness of Purpose" statement that outlines the scope of what one wants and why, when they want it, and the price they are prepared to pay to have it—in very certain terms.

The reason we create this statement is to form an alignment between our desires and our values, between our conscious and subconscious minds, and ultimately this crucial document serves to provide focus, motivation and inspiration.

The first step in building this statement is to gain clarity for what one wants in real terms. We know from Dr. Hill that we are limited only by our ability to conceive and believe in our ideas, and with the right persistent action these ideas can be achieved, as long as the ideas align with natural law.

To think big and outside of our comfort zone, we have to maintain a positive mental attitude. If we are not in this mindset, every idea will be analyzed in terms of why it is not possible rather than why it is. The mind will provide an answer to whatever question is asked. Having a positive mental attitude ensures we ask the right questions so real progress can be made in any endeavor. When challenges arise, Dr. Hill reminds us in chapter one that "every adversity brings with it the seed of an equivalent advantage" as long as we have a positive mental attitude to be aware of this advantage.

Once the statement is created, it does no good unless it is internalized with sufficient emotion with the right attitude. This process of internalizing the desire increases our awareness of new opportunities, people and circumstances that can be acted upon.

Faith

Dr. Hill in chapter two explains that:
"Faith is the head chemist of the mind. When faith is blended with the vibration of thought, the subconscious mind instantly picks up the vibration, translates it into its spiritual equivalent, and transmits it to Infinite Intelligence, as in the case of prayer."

He goes on to say:
"Faith is a state of mind which may be induced, or created by affirmations, or repeated instructions to the subconscious mind, through the principle of autosuggestion."

Based on the above we can see the level of importance associated with faith. Faith gives us the ability to see in our mind's eye the invisible, and what others deem as impossible. We then can maintain our focus and apply our talent and skills to bring forth our dream into physical reality.

To this end, Dr. Hill suggests that when we call upon our subconscious mind, we need to do so as if we are "already in the possession of the material thing which [we] are demanding."

To facilitate the above in a productive manner it is essential that we maintain a consistent and focused positive mental attitude.

Dr. Hill further discusses the importance of self-confidence as a means of nurturing our faith and keeping the burning desire alive.

Self-confidence is the deep belief that you have the right skills, experience and talent to achieve your goals. Self-confidence is the essential ingredient that allows someone to move from having an idea to acting on an idea. Without enough self-confidence no action will ever be taken. With too much self-confidence, unforeseen challenges are likely to occur. Neither case is ideal. However, a benefit of over-confidence is that it leads to action.

Action allows someone to gain experience and get outside his or her comfort zone. A person who is overly confident is likely to misstep—but it is from these missteps that real learning occurs. This of course has to be done carefully with full respect for reality and natural law. Let's analyze how and why a burning desire and a positive mental attitude are both critical to generating self-confidence.

Self-confidence is present when we hold a positive expectation or belief for the future and how it may turn out. The first step to deviate from the status quo is to make a firm decision for change. This step requires courage, and usually comes from reaching a certain pain threshold where enough is enough! The change we want in our life is linked to a positive expectation or belief for how the future will turn out. Without this expectation, self-confidence could not exist. So, to have self-confidence, a prerequisite is to keep the positive mental attitude that the future will be better than the present.

The second step is to get highly relevant specialized knowledge and have enough patience to analyze and integrate the information together in a format favorable to action.

The third step is to find other people who are successfully doing what you want to do. You need role models. To attract these coaches and mentors, it is essential to develop a pleasing personality based on a positive mindset. It is also a must to maintain an unwavering passionate desire.

The fourth step is to apply your knowledge in a meaningful way in the real world. Again, without a positive mental attitude you will repel just about everyone you come in contact with and the possibility of them helping you achieve your desires.

The fifth step is to form a support group that can be leveraged as a mastermind (will be discussed later) to offer ideas, contacts and strategies to help make your desire come true. Again a positive mental attitude is absolutely necessary for harmony with the mastermind or the mastermind will not work to help you.

The last step is to train the mind on how to deal with either a positive or negative outcome. If negative, it is a learning experience. If positive, you can use it to reinforce the belief that one is being successful and making progress. This in turn boosts self-confidence. This awareness of mind is only possible to a highly evolved thinker who maintains a consistent and focused positive mental attitude.

Within the context of discussing self-confidence, Dr. Hill states that *"all impulses of thought have a tendency to clothe themselves in their physical equivalent."* Every step in building self-confidence requires a positive mental attitude beginning with impulses of thought and ending with learning and advancing through taking action.

Autosuggestion

The process of autosuggestion is the volitional act of impressing the definite desire on the subconscious mind so that it can serve as a magnet to attract the people, things and circumstances conducive to reaching our objectives. Autosuggestion conditions the mind to be very alert. It is important to note that the subconscious mind is deductive in nature and will accept as real anything emotionally impressed upon it for a period of time.

Dr. Hill clearly states that:

"[The student] should read aloud twice daily the written statement of your desire for money, and see and feel yourself already in possession of the money! By following these instructions, you communicate the object of your desire directly to your subconscious mind in a spirit of absolute faith.

In order to do this in a productive manner, it is critical to have a positive mental attitude with great expectations for the future while undergoing autosuggestion.

Specialized Knowledge

In today's fast moving ever-changing world, the acquisition of specialized knowledge has never been more important. Dr. Hill explains that:

"The accumulation of great fortune calls for power, and power is acquired through highly organized and intelligently directed specialized knowledge, but that knowledge does not necessarily have to be in the possession of the person who accumulates the fortune."

Let us consider the process for acquiring specialized knowledge. The assimilation of specialized knowledge comes from having meaningful learning experiences. These experiences can occur in isolation or in a group setting. In either case, to learn we must have a desire that motivates us to take action and then be focused and able to avoid distractions. If we are in a negative vibration we cannot be 100% present and therefore the acquisition of specialized knowledge is not very efficient.

Dr. Hill indicated that the "specialized knowledge" does not need to be in the possession of the person who accumulates the fortune. In order to garner the good will of others to share their knowledge as a colleague or as an employee, what we need is an encouraging, pleasing personality that draws their support.

The primary ingredient for a pleasing personality is a positive mental attitude. To be persuasive with others, it is important that we communicate our desire through our enthusiasm, as we explain how we plan to render service to others. By doing so, we are in a position of strength to obtain their support and specialized knowledge because the end objective is worthwhile.

Imagination

The imagination is one of our intellectual assets that sets us apart from other living creatures. Based on our burning desire for what we really want, we have the ability to construct ideas in our mind that take the form of pictures. We then blend these pictures together to represent ideas and form concepts.

Using our imagination is critical to making our life better and helping the world at large. It is only through the power of imagination that new ideas are born, and with them the potential of being, doing and having more abundance in our lives.

We are most imaginative when we have a very clear objective to reach and are in a relaxed positive mindset.

Let's analyze what happens to our level of imagination when we are in a *negative* vibration.

If we say we are "feeling bad," it means we are entertaining a negative thought pattern that is not serving us. At a given point in time, our minds can only focus on a single thought. So, if we are thinking of a negative thought that makes us feel bad, we cannot possibly be fully engaged in using our imagination to make progress. Therefore, a negative mindset limits or sometimes completely kills off the productive use of our imagination.

In order to stand by an idea until it manifests itself into the physical medium, a tremendous positive mindset that is supported by "*determination, definiteness of purpose, the desire to attain the goal and the persistent effort [over a long period is needed].*" Our mindset protects our dreams and ideas from the many "*disappointments, discouragements, temporary defeats, criticism and the constant reminding [from others] that we are wasting our time.*"

The natural mode of operation for the mind is one of peace and tranquility. When we are in a positive frame of mind, we support this natural state, and the mind can then relax and be productive.

Organized Planning

Having an organized plan that can be followed to transmute a desire into a physical result is critical to success and is often overlooked. Dr. Hill supports this statement as he says "*your achievement can be no greater than your plans are sound.*" What does it take to create sound plans? To create a sound plan, the mind must be open and receptive to new ideas that can be integrated together in a logical sequence. To obtain this level of clarity, the mind must be relaxed and alert. In order to have an alert and active mind, we must be focused. To be focused, the mind must reject the many negative vibrations that serve as distractions to the task at hand.

Dr. Hill further explained that in the production of goods and services we must consider "the quality and quantity of service rendered, and the spirit in which it is rendered." Dr. Hill indicated that the spirit of service should be "*construed to mean the habit of agreeable, harmonious conduct which will induce the cooperation from associates and fellow employees.*" In fact, "*Andrew Carnegie stressed this point more than others in connection with his description of the factors which lead to success in the marketing of personal services.*"

Decision

It has been well documented that an "*analysis of several hundred people who had accumulated fortunes well beyond the million dollar mark disclosed the fact that everyone of them had the habit of reaching decisions promptly and of changing these decisions slowly, if and when they were changed. People who fail to accumulate money, without exception, have the habit of reaching decisions, if at all, very slowly and of changing these decisions quickly and often.*"

The question we must ask is, what is the decision making process and how can decisions be made faster? Real decisions represent a course of action that varies from the status quo designed to bring upon a positive change. What mindset must a person be in to embrace the possibility of change? The mindset needed is one with faith that the future condition will be better than the present one. Otherwise, there is no need for change and the decision to make one.

A mindset of positive expectation is a requirement to make a sound decision quickly, and it must be aligned with the burning desire. If and when a decision needs to be changed, it should be assessed in relation to the burning desire and changed carefully.

For complex decisions, the process is to collect and organize relevant data and analyze it methodically. Once the data has been integrated and analyzed, we run various scenarios that forecast the outcome. To accomplish these objectives productively, again, we need a positive and objective mental attitude to ensure the we are making the right decision and not one coming from frustration or anger.

Dr. Hill reminds us that, "Definiteness of decision always requires courage, sometimes very great courage." This is very true, especially when the decision takes us far outside our comfort zone. The further we go outside our comfort zone, the stronger the desire and positive mindset we must have to stay focused in a spirit of faith that everything will work out.

Persistence

Once a decision has been made, persistence is the next ingredient to the success equation. Dr. Hill so eloquently states that *"There may be no heroic connotation to the word persistence, but the quality is to a person's character what carbon is to steel."*

In order to be persistent and have the willpower to be successful, we first must believe success is possible. To believe success is possible we need to have a burning desire that keeps us moving forward and be optimistic that we are on the right path.

Harmonious Mastermind

The notion of a mastermind may be defined as *"Coordination of knowledge and effort, in a spirit of harmony between two or more people, for the attainment of a definite purpose."* A harmonious mastermind is one in which each member is genuinely interested in being a resource to further the advancement of each individual of the mastermind as they know and embrace the concept that givers gain. A mastermind exists to provide support and guidance to each of the members. As Dr. Hill has mentioned above, a mastermind cannot function if less than a spirit of perfect harmony exists across its members. Harmony can only be present when each member of the mastermind exhibits a positive mental attitude. If even a single individual embraces a negative vibration, the overall effect on the mastermind is substantially reduced if not eliminated. With respect to the quote above, Dr. Hill uses the word "definite purpose." A definite purpose can only be formulated if there is a definite desire.

The Mystery of Sex Transmutation

The intimate and powerful emotional experience of sex can only occur between two people who have a deep connection and respect for one another. Transmuting sexual energy involves being able to summon the same enthusiasm and determination and raw energy used in the physical act to give birth to new ideas via our creative imagination. To access the creative imagination we need to increase the rate at which our mind vibrates based on the various mind stimulants outlined by Dr. Hill, with sexual energy being the most powerful. Dr. Hill clearly states that *the emotion of sex contains the secret of creative ability.* In order to unleash this creative ability, we have to maintain a positive mental attitude to: a) be with someone who can truly inspire us and b) be able to effectively channel this energy into a worthwhile and productive endeavor. Without this positive mindset—the productive transmutation of sexual energy cannot and will not occur.

The Subconscious Mind

The subconscious mind, or subjective mind, serves as a giant database that records everything the conscious mind or objective mind passes along to it. The objective mind collects a wide variety of information through the five senses, and classifies it so it can be stored and recalled at a later time.

To a large extent, your view of the world is shaped by the positive or negative mental attitude you maintained in the past as you labeled your experiences either "good or bad." This attitude shaped your perceptions and the stories you told yourself about what is true and real. It is important to realize there is only one reality, but there are many perceptions of this reality. These interpretations or perceptions are to a large extent influenced by our attitude.

To form new beliefs and paradigms about ourselves and the world at large requires a very strong positive mental attitude to combat the years of the negative influence we have allowed to creep into our subconscious mind by not staying alert.

Real change requires a burning desire and determination to instill a new belief or paradigm to replace the one inside of us that holds us to our current level of performance.

Dr. Hill further describes the seven positive emotions that can be used to influence the subconscious mind:

1. The emotion of DESIRE
2. The emotion of FAITH
3. The emotion of LOVE
4. The emotion of SEX
5. The emotion of ENTHUSIASM
6. The emotion of ROMANCE
7. The emotion of HOPE

He then outlines the seven major negative emotions:
1. The emotion of FEAR
2. The emotion of JEALOUSY
3. The emotion of HATRED
4. The emotion of REVENGE
5. The emotion of GREED
6. The emotion of SUPERSTITION
7. The emotion of ANGER

Without exception can you see that all seven positive emotions could not be possible without a positive mental attitude? Can you also see each of the seven negative emotions can only exist in the absence of a positive mental attitude?

Concluding Thoughts

Napoleon Hill intended that his secret be discovered by the astute student. He felt the work involved to uncover this mystery would serve the student well, and correspondingly be more meaningful once found. As we have discussed the major chapters in the book *Think and Grow Rich* I have shown that each concept could not be possible without the secret ingredient which stated again is:

A person must cultivate and maintain a burning desire for success that is channeled in a productive manner through a consistent and focused positive mental attitude at all times, and under all conditions.

Now that you have the Master Key, use it wisely to confidently move forward and build a life worthy of the greatness within you!

About Ray Stendall

Ray Stendall is one of America's leading authorities on the development of human potential and personal effectiveness. He is a dynamic and entertaining speaker with a wonderful ability to inform and inspire audiences toward peak performance and higher levels of achievement. Ray also provides results oriented Internet Marketing and Business Consulting Services. He can be reached through his website, http://www.RayStendall.com

5

Take Control of Your Destiny

by Jim Rohrbach

Napoleon Hill claims to have embedded the "secret" in *Think and Grow Rich* no fewer than a hundred times. He states in the preface:

> *"Somewhere, as you read, the secret to which I refer will jump from the page and stand boldly before you, if you are ready for it! When it appears, you will recognize it. Whether you receive the sign in the first or the last chapter, stop for a moment when it presents itself and raise your glass to toast your epiphany."*

After numerous readings myself way back when (frustrated that I had not yet figured it out!), I carefully read both the first and the last chapter and realized that the wily Hill revealed what that secret is on the very last page:

> *"The master key is intangible but it is powerful! It is the privilege of creating, in your own mind, a burning desire for a definite form of riches. There is no penalty for the use of the key, but*

there is a price you must pay if you do not use it. The price is failure. There is a reward of stupendous proportions if you put the key to use. It is the satisfaction that comes to all who conquer self and force life to pay whatever is asked."

In other words, we all have the freedom (and the responsibility, if we'll take it) to make up our mind about exactly what we want. Thus we take control of our own fate, become the creator of our own destiny.

Although it's been years since this light bulb went on for me, I'm grateful that Napoleon Hill made me work to uncover the secret—anything worth having is worth working for!

About Jim Rohrbach

Success Skills Coach Jim Rohrbach, "The Personal Fitness Trainer for Your Business," coaches business owners, entrepreneurs and sales professionals on growing their clientele. He has helped hundreds of individuals to achieve their goals since he developed his first coaching program in 1982. To arrange a Free Consultation with Jim, go to www .SuccessSkills.com.

6

Finding the formula for Success in Think and Grow Rich

by Judith B. Arcy, Ph. D.

MEMPHIS, TENNESSEE

Those of us who subscribe to Dr. Napoleon Hill's methodology for success are often asked, "Where did you find this 'formula for success' that Dr. Hill claims is in, *THINK AND GROW RICH?*" While Dr. Hill lets us know almost immediately that his book contains what we need to become rich; he does not claim there is a secret formula hidden in the book. He does say what we need to know is in the book. I did not have a light-bulb moment that caused me to jump-up and shout I've got it! I feel the formula for a rich life is within the words and is an individual equation. While all basic formulas for a successful life have common elements, the key is the individual recognition of the arrangement of the elements for each reader.

We all recognize that the seventeen principles are a synthesis of Dr. Hill's twenty year research under the guidance of Andrew Carnegie. It is by far the earliest of the self-help, positive mental attitude messages and the foundation for all of the contemporary literature for organizing one's search for success.

Dr. Hill begins our journey with the seemingly simple statement that, "thoughts are things" and very powerful things. He leads us to the fundamental or base line of a formula for success which is having definiteness of purpose. We are advised to value our thoughts, mentally explore our desires and define what we personally feel is success.

Dr. Hill believed that desire is the starting point of all achievement. Use your mind and emotions to find your dominating desire—perhaps writing thoughts down to see what you keep returning to when your mind is free. This may sound like a daunting task. It involves searching your innermost self with no reservations, to explore your definition of success. When you believe you can achieve whatever you desire and develop feelings so strong that you put it in writing for daily review, you have found a definiteness of purpose.

Recommendation is made to be positive, keep focused on what you want and away from thoughts about what isn't desired or shouldn't be experienced. Daily review of definiteness of purpose allows us to stay focused, make modifications when needed and re-energize our progress to success.

Dr. Hill's short stories of people who achieved success made the concepts more concrete to me and gave a real life perspective to often intangible ideas.

I especially like Hill's statement that "Faith is the head chemist of the mind." He believed that faith is the link between the conscious and subconscious. One's faith in a well thought out definiteness of purpose leads to enhanced self-confidence, purposeful planning and acceptance that desires will be realities. Faith is the conduit between desire and the reality that ultimately leads us to riches, be they monetary or intrinsic.

The majority of my professional life has been spent in the education community. I have taught pre-school through university. For over twenty years, I was a civil servant in the United States Department of Defense assigned to the Navy Recruiting Command.

Beginning with my first day of teaching, I found that by helping young people build their own self confidence, I enhanced my own confidence and also got pleasure in seeing young citizens become happy, productive adults. Sometimes this didn't happen, which caused me sadness laced with hope. In the beginning of my career, I didn't formally identify my definite purpose in life as helping people become happy and productive through education, but I was always drawn to educational opportunities and experiences. I feel good when I see my students (adults or children) succeed. That enriches my life.

A lesson I learned early was to be open to new and sometimes unusual opportunities. This is part of Dr. Hill's concept of faith. That is what led to my exciting and non-traditional career as an educator with the United States Navy.

I thought I had nicely settled into an academic life in a wonderful university community. I was teaching young energetic students who saw an ever expanding world open for them. Their energy and anticipation were contagious. As a grant writer and Upward Bound director, I had merged two of my favorite things (writing and teaching) with my need to help people. Travel has always been a part of my definition of purpose. An opportunity to participate in one of the Navy's Educator Orientation Visits came my way and changed my life.

This wasn't as accidental as it may have appeared. The type of grant writing that I did used the concept of masterminding both within the university and through a professional organization of equal opportunity professional educators. Part of our tasking was to develop career awareness opportunities for our secondary and university students.

The Navy's purpose for the visits was to acquaint educators regarding the career and education opportunities in the Navy. All of my students came from low-income families and had usually not had much exposure to a variety of careers outside of their communities. With the blessing of the Dean, I was off to San Diego with the Navy! We toured aviation squadrons, surface ships, submarines and classrooms. I learned how much sailors used their junior and senior high school mathematics and what an awesome amount of responsibility is given to these young people. Everything you need to keep a small city running is needed on a ship. An aircraft carrier has more crew members than the population of the small town where I grew up. I came home with much knowledge, enhanced respect for our military professionals and opportunities for my students. All needed help funding their college education and now I could add another opportunity to their list of possibilities.

Less than a month later, I received a telephone call from the Navy asking me to apply for a position as Education Services Specialist at their Kansas City Recruiting District. My responsibilities would include visiting secondary schools and universities in a three state area, qualifying applicants for special ratings, ensuring applicants had authentic education documents and helping educators to understand the Navy and helping the Navy personnel understand civilians. The position included taking educators on visits, like the one I had experienced, at Navy facilities all over the United States.

This opportunity offered me the chance to do many of the things I had on my "someday list." I would still have contact with high school and college students who needed help making career decisions, would still have writing opportunities and I would travel! It was bittersweet to leave my students and the comfort and freedom of the academic community, but I was excited to have a chance to be an educator in a non-traditional manner. My children, all in college, encouraged me to do it—and I did!

During my twenty plus years as an "EdSpec," I lived in Kansas City, Kansas and worked in Kansas City, Missouri, then Chicago, Il and Memphis, TN. I became the education advisor to the Admiral and traveled to most of the United States and met hundreds of interesting young people who are proud of what they have accomplished.

I was able to observe successful people in the civilian and military genre. The seventeen principles documented by Napoleon Hill are most evident in both communities. The outstanding, successful members depend on teamwork, masterminding, going the extra mile, self-discipline, enthusiasm, accurate thinking, controlled attention, personal initiative, creativity and pleasing personality to lead and follow. Additionally maintenance of sound health is a condition of employment for military and an absolute necessity for sustained success in any education scenario.

The above listed principles seem to be intertwined. People with a pleasing personality, which has been defined by some as not being negative, may find a successful experience which can lead to masterminding. A person with controlled attention, personal initiative and accurate thinking may be called upon for teamwork because they have knowledge needed to implement a concept. This also leads to masterminding. The possible combinations of the seventeen principles are lengthy and each makes it easier for an individual to develop and refine a definiteness of purpose with a flexible plan for success which can lead to whatever that person considers riches.

Some people have been known to shy away from a discussion of Cosmic Habitforce. I feel it is the basis for the other principles and is the motivation behind developing a definiteness of purpose. There has and continues to be a mostly quiet spiritual guidance for me. Although I sometimes didn't recognize it immediately, I don't think there are coincidences in life, but opportunities for us to use our free will to do the right thing. I had an often suppressed desire to travel and by a series of "fortunate decisions" I was able to combine travel with my profession, in which I am still active in a more relaxed manner. I am retired, but still teaching in yet another non-traditional manner.

One of the most interesting people I met as I traveled the country, visiting public and private schools, was the Principal of a small Indiana high school. As sometimes happens, we seemed to develop an immediate friendship as well as professional relationship. Shortly before I retired she called me and said she was now the director of the Napoleon Hill World Learning Center. I told her I was going to retire and she said, "Good, now you can go to Malaysia with us. I need another speaker." That was the beginning of my new adventure in education.

As is *not* often the case, I was speechless. Malaysia was not on my "bucket list" simply because I had not thought it through very well. Judy Williamson, by her support, helped me revisit my definiteness of purpose and become an active advocate for Napoleon Hill. My experience in two very different parts of my own society has given me the opportunity to see that Dr. Hill's ideas are workable in any situation.

Through the Napoleon Hill Foundation, I am still able to teach, travel and meet the wonderful, interesting people all over the world.

I have learned that there are many ways to be rich. For some money is the most important concept. For others it is having people to reach out to; for others it is the freedom to do something in addition to their career. I feel we all give and receive gifts (or riches, if you prefer) daily. I briefly held a lady's hand during Mass one day—and she thanked me afterward. We didn't know each other and have never seen each other again. It just seemed the right thing to do and once again the cosmic habit force was there to create a sense of order. I am daily amazed how easy it can be to make a difference in someone's life and especially my own. I consider that one of my riches.

One of the many gifts available from *Think and Grow Rich* is the opportunity to read it again and again. Each time you read it you will find new treasures and opportunity to refine existing goals or set new goals. Not every goal can be accomplished on the first try. When set-backs occur, Hill recommends that we look at the positives that did occur, rework the less than successful strategies and try again. His prime examples are Thomas Edison and Walt Disney.

The movie Forest Gump provides a visual example of many of Dr. Hill's documented principles. Even though Forest recognized that he was "not a bright man," as he told Jenny, he listened to his mother who told him to look within himself, find what he liked to do and always do his best. The famous box of chocolates statement holds true for everyone. Forest learned from adversity, early in his life, that honesty and caring for others helped him meet his goals. Forest made the most of his vast and varied opportunities. He always went the extra mile, had a pleasing personality, and applied faith, which eventually led him to what he really desired.

The "big secret" we "need to get" is not a simple formula for success. I believe that it is the actualization of a concept most of us learned early in life, regardless of our religion or faith. *"Do unto others, as you would have them do unto you."* We need to recognize the talents God has given us, realize that we need to set high goals both personally and professionally, define them, develop and execute a plan using the seventeen principles and enjoy what we are doing. The foundation of a successful plan is personal honor and the ability to love our fellow humans, even when we aren't always easy to love.

The listing of the successful people in the front of *Think and Grow Rich* is not only a list of Dr. Hill's research subjects, but a listing of people who respected and genuinely cared about humanity. They all had a commitment to bettering mankind. Dr. Hill explains, "The peculiar thing about the secret is that those who once acquire it and use it, find themselves literally swept on to success with but little effort and they never again submit to failure!" He goes on to say that there is no such thing as something for nothing and the secret to success cannot be bought. It can only be found by those who are intentionally searching for it.

The best reward we can give to ourselves is the gift of realization. We need to humbly appreciate our gifts from Cosmic Habit Force and our accomplishments so we can continue growing to be emotionally and spiritually rich and that will make a better world for all.

Good hunting! I am confident you will find your secret formula within the pages of *Think and Grow Rich*.

About Judith Arcy

Judith Arcy, Ph. D., is a professional education consultant in Memphis, Tennessee. She is an experienced grant writer, government education advisor, public and private sector teacher and a certified Napoleon Hill Instructor. She finds the 17 Principles for Success, enumerated by Dr. Hill, to be guiding lights professionally and personally. You may reach her through her e-mail: judyarcy@bellsouth.net.

7

Be, Do, Have!

by Shane Morand

OAKVILLE, ONTARIO CANADA

Although I consider myself an amateur on the topic of Napoleon Hill's classic book *Think and Grow Rich* here is my story and what I believe the secret he referred to so many times in the book.

I will never forget the day I stumbled into a copy of *Think and Grow Rich.* This was the day my life was positively changed forever in ways I could not have previously imagined. I was 19 years old and had just started my first job as a Production Coordinator (gopher) with a major printing company in Ottawa, Canada. My total salary before taxes was a whopping $10,000 per year. Just to put things into perspective, I remember every 2 weeks I would go to the local bank and deposit my paycheck of $284.00. Every 2 weeks!

I had no special skills that were out of the ordinary, other than I was a pretty good Hockey player and was drafted in the first round (second pick overall) playing junior hockey. I did however, have an extraordinary DESIRE to make a success of my life and I believe the day I started to read Napoleon Hill's all time best selling business book in history, *Think and Grow Rich*, was the day everything started to change for me . . . it was as though Napoleon Hill himself handed me a blank check and the amount I now had the power to write on that check was totally in my control. And I knew it . . . I believed, I too could *Think and Grow Rich.*

The Year Was 1982

The advances in technology that began in previous years continued to gain momentum in 1982 with the release of the Commodore 64 computer and the first CD player by Sony. The shift in technology is so significant that Time Magazine names "The Computer" as the person of the year. Other big news items included the opening of Disney's Epcot Center, the dedication of the Vietnam Veterans' Memorial, the Tylenol scare, the death of John Belushi, the birth of Prince William and the first reported cases of AIDS in Canada. It was a great year in movies with ET, Fast Times, the Wall, all at the box office. Michael Jackson ruled the music scene and the airwaves with Thriller, which became the best selling album of all in time. 1982 . . . I embrace you with open arms, as it was the year I started to read Napoleon Hill's classic *Think and Grow Rich.* It was the year everything would now change for me.

The Secret?

I remember opening the book reading Napoleon Hill's *Think and Grow Rich.* Back then, I was furiously devouring every page and even though I couldn't recall most of the details in that 1937 classic then, a very curious statement Napoleon

Hill repeated several times stuck with me. . . . He said that there was a *"secret." "A secret? What secret? Where is the secret? I need to find the secret! How will I know when I've discovered the secret? Will this Secret make a difference in my life? Where the heck is the secret?"* He said it was on every page but it would only appear when the student was ready to discover the secret. *"Well of course I am ready! I am 19 years old and I need that secret"* . . . so I began to read the book, then I re-read the book again, and again and again and I noticed something so interesting that it still gives me goose bumps when I think of it even today.

I noticed that every time I read and re-read *Think and Grow Rich*, it was as though someone had added new pages of information to my book, new concepts to my book, new life lessons to my book, new strategies to my book that had not been there the last time I read *Think and Grow Rich* even though I may have just finished re-reading the book a few days earlier! How could that be?

No matter how many times I re-read *Think and Grow Rich* I would always believe that I NOW knew the secret Napoleon Hill was referring to. BUT if I now knew the secret then why did the secret change for me with every new reading?

This was my indicator that I did not in fact know or understand the secret, however, I was absolutely determined that I would discover, on my own, this secret and I was single-minded to do it in this lifetime!

There was one concept and an important idea that stuck with me . . . *"Everyone is capable of achieving anything his or her mind can conceive and believe."* In fact, I was so fascinated with that earth shattering piece of information and the many terms Napoleon Hill mentioned in the book—such as DESIRE, FAITH, PERSISTENCE, IMAGINATION, GOING

THE EXTRA MILE, AUTO SUGGESTION,—that I started sharing these concepts with everyone I knew. In other words if I knew them, I had probably mentioned these fascinating concepts to them.

I thought "that" was the hidden secret. I knew the bits and pieces. But I never really got the big picture. The secret to me only came to me after reading the book over and over and over until I thought I had practically memorized every chapter in the entire book. . . . Then I re-read it again. And I finally got it! More on that later.

The hidden secret is in fact on every page and I have already given you several clues as to what the secret is (for me). The secret is, in my opinion, of course, every reader of *Think and Grow Rich* has the opportunity to discover for themselves the secret Napoleon Hill referred to. (*Don't be lazy now!*)

Let's fast forward . . . since reading Napoleon Hill's classic *Think and Grow Rich* for the very first time, 6 months later I purchased my first house at the age of 19 . . . 6 short years later at the age of 25, I became the youngest Vice President of Sales and Marketing in the history of a major printing company in Ottawa, Canada (the Nation's Capital). I helped launch the world's first television network dedicated to success, helped assemble a team that broke every sales record in the history of a 24 year old (NYSE) publically traded company, built a few multi-million dollar enterprises, met the woman of my dreams—my wife Josie and I have travelled all over the world to places like, Bali, Singapore, Jamaica, Philippines, Thailand, Japan, Ireland, Netherlands, Germany, Costa Rica, Dominica, Mexico, Hawaii, just to name a few. AND we have met some of the most amazing people we now get to call our friends and we have enjoyed a heck of a lot of FUN! And, most recently, I have had the distinct honor of being invited to write the foreword to the historical collectors' edition of. . . . You guessed it . . . *Think and Grow Rich!*

I am not writing this to impress you but to impress upon you that there is a secret in the book and it is on every page and if you are not living your dreams and reaching your highest goals, chances are you have simply not internalized the secret . . . YET! And . . . here is the most important question you must answer for yourself . . . When would <u>NOW</u> be an excellent time to DECIDE to change that?

And What's Most Amazing

What's most amazing is that the secret is on every page just like Napoleon Hill said it was . . . before I share the secret; let me first ask you to recall a major achievement you accomplished in your life . . .

Think of a specific achievement or accomplishment you feel very proud of right now in this moment. Get a clear picture whether it's the car you drive, the job you have, the house you live in, perhaps it's an award you earned, or something very special you were able to purchase or maybe it's a once-in-a-lifetime vacation you were able to enjoy. There may be many things in your life you are extremely proud of but for now I want you to think of just ONE!

And to demonstrate the secret in a way you can experience it you need to be crystal clear on the specific achievement, promotion, accomplishment you are most proud of right now. Are you thinking about it right now? If not, do not proceed. . . . Got it?

OK, here goes . . . as you think of this one achievement or accomplishment, you will discover you have already been using the secret and it is in fact on every page and that I have already given several clues as to what it is in this chapter so here goes:

THINK and GROW RICH

That's the secret that is on every page, that is the secret that you have already been using a little or a lot depending on your current circumstances, that is the secret that you can purposely use to BE, DO and HAVE practically anything you want, that is the secret that you knowingly or even unknowingly used to accomplish the one thing or accomplishment you have been thinking about in the last few minutes.

THINK

Before you achieved your accomplishment did you not THINK about it over and over and over until you were crystal clear on what it was you wanted? Did you not picture it as though it was already a reality long before you achieved your desired outcome? Of course you did, because everything starts with a THOUGHT!

The chair you are sitting on was someone's THOUGHT long before it became a chair. The book you are holding in your hands right now was the author's THOUGHT long before it became a book; the clothes you are wearing were all THOUGHTS in someone's mind long before you walked into the store to purchase them.

And in my opinion, here is the coolest part . . . you may or may not control much around you, however, the ONLY thing you have 100% control of are your THOUGHTS! Think about that for a few seconds! Most people you know have never considered that they control their own thoughts, that they are responsible for their own thoughts, that at any-time they can make a decision to take responsibility for their thoughts and create for themselves a bigger, brighter and more fantastic future starting now simply by taking step 1 which is to THINK about what it is that you really want in life. So what are you THINKING?

When you get excited about what you are THINKING about, chances are you will start to take ACTION on those thoughts and move in the direction of those thoughts too. As you start taking action and moving closer to your desired goal, you may notice your confidence starts to GROW no matter how small the goal or the target. As your confidence grows, you will take more action towards your goal and as you take more actions your results will increase, as the results increase, confidence grows and as confidence grows you will take more action and move even closer to your goal. . . . I could go on, but I think you've got the point.

EVERYTHING you want to BE, DO and HAVE starts with Your THOUGHTS. So in my humble opinion, (I would like to remind you I am an amateur on this subject) I believe the secret that Napoleon Hill was referring to was that THOUGHTS are very real, thoughts are things and I believe he gave us the biggest clue of all when he said,

"Whatever the mind of man can conceive and believe, it can achieve."

THINK big, dream big and stay focused on what you want to BE, DO and HAVE and remember this . . . If you THINK you CAN or if you THINK you CAN'T . . . you are right!

About Shane Morand

Shane Morand is the Co-Founder and Global Master Distributor for OrGano Gold International, the "Healthier" Coffee Company and has been enthusiastically introducing the world to Healthier Coffee since April of 2004. Shane understands goal achieving and success. He has been reading and applying Napoleon Hill's success principles since he was 19 years old. Shane is married to his wife Josie and they enjoy traveling around the world meeting like-minded people. You can reach him through his website: www.ShaneMorand.com

The secret to which I refer cannot be had without a price, although the price is far less than its value. It cannot be had at any price by those who are not intentionally searching for it. It cannot be given away, it cannot be purchased for money, for the reason that it comes in two parts. One part is already in possession of those who are ready for it.

—NAPOLEON HILL

8

Belief—The Secret that Hides on the Pages of Think and Grow Rich

by Gail Brooks

LECLAIRE, IOWA

According to Napoleon Hill, the *secret* is mentioned no less than a hundred times throughout the book *Think and Grow Rich*, and at least once in every chapter. The *secret*, states Mr. Hill, is the Master Key that unlocks the door to life's bountiful riches. It is intangible but it is powerful!

Napoleon Hill said, "I have never known anyone who was inspired to use the secret who did not achieve noteworthy success in his chosen calling. I have never known any person to distinguish himself, or to accumulate riches of any consequence, without possession of the secret."

I believe that the intangible and powerful key to success is belief!

Every page of *Think and Grow Rich* admonishes the reader to BELIEVE! Every chapter emphasizes the importance of *belief* and provides the road map and individual steps for building one's *belief*.

Webster defines *belief* as the mental act, condition, or habit of placing trust or confidence in a person or thing. It is the mental acceptance or conviction in the truth or actuality of something. It is something *believed* or accepted as true. Faith is defined as a confident *belief* in the truth, value or trustworthiness of a person, idea, or a thing. Faith is in fact, *belief* that does not rest on logical proof or material evidence. Faith is loyalty—allegiance to a person or thing. *Belief* is persistent and consistent faith in action!

To be successful, you must *believe* that the laws detailed in *Think and Grow Rich* apply to everyone—even you—regardless of your race, your religion, your heredity, your economic status or your past, present or current circumstances. To become successful, you must have *faith* in, coupled with the courage to use and implement, each of the principles presented in *Think and Grow Rich* into your life. To be successful, you must believe:

+ That you have been endowed with the seeds of greatness
+ That you were born for a purpose
+ That you are worthy of success
+ That the resources you require will be made available to you
+ That you can provide a valuable service
+ That you are free and able to pursue your dream by whatever means available so long as it is honest, legal, moral and does not violate the rights of others
+ That as an American citizen, you have all of the freedom and all of the opportunities required to accumulate all of the riches, however you define riches, that you require

+ That you have the opportunity and the ability to render a useful service and to collect riches in proportion to the value of that service
+ That you possess the ability to reach quick and definite decisions
+ That you have a mind and a brain of your own and you alone possess the ability to use it
+ That you have the courage to dream big dreams and achieve them
+ In the power of the Universe and Infinite Intelligence
+ That every failure brings with it the seed of an equivalent advantage
+ In your ability to create and carry out an action plan
+ In yourself to aim high and set high goals regardless of what others may say or do to persuade you to do or believe otherwise
+ That there is a magnificent reward for all who choose to take control of their destiny
+ That persistence, concentration of effort, and definiteness of purpose are major sources for achievement—each of which is impossible without *belief* in the fact that YOU CAN!!!

According to Napoleon Hill, "There are millions of people who *believe* themselves 'doomed' to poverty and failure, because of some strange force over which they *believe* they have no control. They are the creators of their own 'misfortunes' because they *believe* they will fail. As a result, the subconscious mind picks up that *belief* and translates it into its physical equivalent."

I *believe* that I can achieve whatever my mind can conceive and *believe*. How about you?

How I Came to Believe

My first encounter with Napoleon Hill and the concept of *belief* in oneself began in 2003. At that time in my life I owned a small graphic design and communications firm in Moline, Illinois. One of my clients was the Rock Island Housing Authority (RIHA), a local public housing authority (PHA). As a PHA, their primary mission is to provide housing to people who have incomes of 30% or below the Area Median Income (AMI). However, RIHA was also very interested in expanding their effectiveness by implementing what the federal government refers to as Family Self-Sufficiency (FSS) programs. In addition, they wanted to move toward economic independence by becoming more entrepreneurial and develop new mixed-income housing to satisfy the housing needs of a broad-based market. To lay the ground work for their plan, they required what they called, an *Asset Management Plan* which, ultimately became a large part of their twenty-year strategic plan. I was part of the team that wrote that plan.

As part of the writing process, I began to research other self-sufficiency programs to determine the best process for implementation. I also looked at many of the government studies regarding the philosophy of mixed-income developments, deconcentration, and the effectiveness of self-sufficiency programming in general. It is important to note that most federally funded FSS programming is geared toward adults.

At the same time in my life, I became an Independent Business Owner in a multi-level marketing corporation. As part of that business, I subscribe to a Professional Development Program (PDP). The corporation sends me a success-based book and a series of motivational audios to listen to each month. Many of the books are based on the teachings of Napoleon

Hill, including *Think and Grow Rich* and Dale Carnegie's *How to Win Friends & Influence People*. As part of the PDP program, I received a book entitled, *The Magic Ladder of Success*. The book is a condensed version of the seventeen principles of personal success developed by Napoleon Hill. The book was published by the Napoleon Hill Foundation in conjunction with the Napoleon Hill World Learning Center.

As I read the book, I kept thinking about the research I had done regarding poverty and the social challenges associated with federally subsidized housing and the self-sufficiency programming that would be required to break that cycle. What struck me was the Thirty Most Common Causes of Failure listed in the back of the book. According to Napoleon Hill, an unfavorable hereditary foundation stands at the head of the list as the cause of any failure, or temporary defeat. "Bad breeding," in his words, "is a handicap against which there is but little remedy, and it is one for which the individual, unfortunately, is not responsible."

It was then that it *hit me!* We were targeting the wrong group. Based on Napoleon Hill's theory, it was too late for the majority of the adults living in poverty to change their perception of themselves and their life circumstances. However, if we could somehow reach out to the children, and instill in them some measure of hope, and provide them with the tools they required to break the cycle, there was a chance—a real opportunity to have a positive impact on hundreds of young lives!

The second thing that struck me was the fact that this goes much farther and much deeper and affects more people than just those living in subsidized housing. We—each and every one of us—*are* whoever we *believe* ourselves to be. If we *believe* we are failures, in whatever aspect of life you can think of, then we are. If we *believe* we can become successful and transform that *belief* into action plans supported by faith and actually *act* on that faith, we can become successful.

People become successful because they *believe* that they can. They *believe* that they have the ability and resources to overcome any obstacle they face—including "bad breeding." They *believe* that every failure carries with it a lesson that they must learn regardless of their past, present or perceived future circumstances. They *believe* that with persistence and a positive mental attitude, whatever they require to accomplish their goal will be supplied to them. *They believe!*

Napoleon Hill said, "Thoughts are things, and powerful things at that, when they are mixed with definiteness of purpose, persistence, and a burning desire (*belief*) for their translation into riches, or other material objects."

Mr. Hill illustrates his point with a story about Mr. Thomas Edison and a "tramp" named Edwin Barnes. According to Hill, Barnes literally *thought* himself into a partnership with the great Edison! He thought himself into a fortune. He had nothing to start with, except the capacity to know (*believe*) what he wanted, and the determination to stand by that desire until he realized it.

Barnes held a confident *belief* in his ability to achieve his goal. To further illustrate the fact that *belief* is indeed the *secret*, note Mr. Edison's statement on the subject, "I had learned from years of experience with men, that when a man really desires a thing so deeply (*believes in it so strongly*), that he is willing to stake his entire future on a single turn of the wheel in order to get it, he is sure to win.

Napoleon Hill sums it up beautifully when he says, "We refuse to *believe* that which we do not understand. We foolishly *believe* that our own limitations are the proper measure of limitations." He further states, "We are the masters of our fate, the captains of our souls, because we have the power to control our thoughts."

Napoleon Hill teaches us that there are no limitations to the mind except those we acknowledge. Both poverty and riches are the offspring of our thoughts. What we think ultimately becomes what we *believe*. Mr. Hill admonishes us to *believe* when he says, "You may as well know right here, that you can never have riches in great quantities unless you can work yourself into a white heat of *desire* for money, and actually *believe* that you will possess it."

According to Napoleon Hill, "No one is ready for a thing until he *believes* he can acquire it." When Edwin Barnes climbed down from the freight train in Orange, N.J., he may have resembled a tramp, but his *thoughts* were those of a king! His desire was not a hope! It was not a wish! It was a keen, pulsating desire, which transcended everything else. It was definite. Edwin Barnes *believed* he would succeed.

Napoleon Hill says, "If the thing you wish to do is right, and *you believe in it*, go ahead and do it! There is nothing, right or wrong, which *belief*, plus burning desire, cannot make real."

We have within us; the power to *believe and achieve*!

The Journey of a Thousand Miles Begins with a Single Step

The realization that the RIHA self-sufficiency efforts, however well meaning, were targeting the wrong audience, was a revelation that so moved me, that I immediately picked up the phone and called the number listed in the back of *The Magic Ladder of Success.* When the Director of the Napoleon Hill World Learning Center, Ms. Judith Williamson, answered the phone, I knew I was on the right track.

I explained who I was and told her about the project that I was working on and that it suddenly had *hit me* that what we really needed was a program to help low-income children understand that they were born with a purpose! I wanted to devise a way, a means, and a "program" that would nurture the dreams of each of these kids. I wanted to help them discover that whatever their circumstances, they deserved their dreams. That they had a right to pursue them—whatever they may be! I wanted to find a way to teach these newly discovered principles to the children living in public housing! I wanted to *arm* them with the tools required for success, and I wanted the Napoleon Hill World Learning Center to develop the program and sprinkle the magic fairy dust required over each of the kids to make it happen!

It sounded like a workable plan to me.

Sadly, I was informed that no-such curriculum existed, but the World Learning Center would assist me if *I* wanted to *pursue* the idea and *develop and implement* the program *myself.*

What's up with that! I thought. I'm not a teacher! I can't spell curriculum much less write one! They were the experts! They were already writing this stuff! I had NO idea where to start. I had a thousand reasons why *I could not.* Sure, I *believed* in the concept and I certainly *believed* that *they* could do it—but I did not *believe* that *I* could do it.

In *Think and Grow Rich,* Mr. Hill teaches us that, "if you lack *belief* in your purpose, the crystallization of your desire along with your ability to turn that desire into action will be impossible. Your ability to overcome adversity and to develop alternate action plans will also be hindered without the *belief* that your goal is worthy of continued pursuit. To be successful in any endeavor, you *must believe* that you are worthy of success and that you will ultimately be successful."

I believed that I was completely incapable of creating such a program. I hadn't even started the project and I had already set myself up for complete failure!

According to Napoleon Hill, "Financial independence, riches, desirable business and professional positions are not within reach of the person who neglects or refuses to except, plan, and demand these things."

It was then that Judy encouraged me to learn more about the principles myself so that I was in a position to develop and implement the program and accomplish my newly discovered *definiteness of purpose.*

Deeds, and not words, are what count most. I had to make a decision.

I did just that. I completed the Distance Learning Program and developed an action plan that set me on a path to bring me closer to my intended goal. But, that did not happen overnight. There were other obstacles besides my insecurities and fear to overcome. First, there was no federal funding to implement the program—so it could not be developed or implemented under the umbrella of the housing authority.

Second, my intention was to introduce the new success-based program in an afterschool setting. I could not envision main stream academia implementing a program based on *Napoleon Hill's 17 Principles of Personal Success.*

Third, there was no money to fund the program and nobody was interested in picking it up on their own. That meant that I needed to find somebody willing to both learn and teach the class for free and I certainly did not envision that happening! Plus, I did not anticipate funding to appear unless I personally went out and found it. But in spite of it all, I persisted, however half heartedly.

Based on Napoleon Hill's *Think and Grow Rich*, the basis of persistence is the power of will—which can be driven only by one's *belief* that they can and will accomplish their purpose. The majority of people who are ready to throw their aims and purposes overboard, and give up at the first sign of opposition, or misfortune lack faith. They lack *belief* that they have the power to overcome any obstacle laid out before them.

"The starting point of all achievement is desire. Weak desires bring weak results." I had weak desire.

The Missing Connecting Link

Sometime later, Judy invited me to attend an Open House at the World Learning Center at Purdue Calumet in Hammond, Indiana. While there, I met some people that expressed an interest in my idea for an afterschool program based on *Napoleon Hill's 17 Principles for Personal Achievement*. They also thought that by working together, we could find the funding required to implement the program in the Gary, Indiana school district. Of course the challenge was that the whole program was still an "idea." I had not actually written any curriculum. I was still (just) thinking about what a great idea it was and how cool it would be if somebody bought into it and (sort of) did the work for me.

I had "poverty thinking" that was based on fear of failure. While I was a very capable writer, I had never written school curriculum and I was afraid that I would not be good at it and I would (therefore) sabotage the program before I ever got it off the ground. Of course I had already sabotaged the program with my inactivity and fear. My fear of criticism had destroyed my initiative, and discouraged the use of my imagination.

In the chapter on the Subconscious Mind, Napoleon Hill teaches us that anybody can wish for riches, and most people do, but very few know that a definite plan, plus a burning desire for wealth, are the only dependable means of accumulating wealth—or accomplishing one's purpose.

I also lacked persistence. I had been doing a lot of wishing, but had not implemented any kind of meaningful action plan. But that was about to change. I was now on the spot to produce something. After much conversation, it was decided that we needed a proposal. Some sort of a document that provided a reasonably intelligent overview of the program coupled with its value for the schools that would potentially incorporate it into their afterschool program. We also needed to consider the value for the students that would participate in the program. This was the kind of writing I could handle! I knew how to do this and I was good at it! And so the process began.

As Napoleon Hill would say, happiness is found in DOING not merely in POSSESSING (or thinking about doing). I went back to the action plan that I had developed during my certification process and found it to be sound, so I dusted it off and began anew. I had overcome a huge obstacle, but it was not the last one—not by a long shot.

We generated a lot of interest in the Gary area. Everybody we talked to loved the concept and told us that they were ready to implement the program based on the availability of funding. So there it was again. Everybody loved the idea so long as it came fully funded and provided a stipend for the instructors. But no funding was available. Nobody wanted to go out on a limb for a non-academically based program.

I was frustrated with the Gary school system, but this time I was not about to set the program aside. I had a solid proposal and I knew I could "sell" the idea to somebody! And so I lamented to a friend. She happened to belong to a local Rock Island, Illinois Rotary Club and they happened to sponsor a local elementary school. The sponsorship included providing school supplies to kids who needed them, buying dictionaries and other books and a variety of other supportive services including the funding of some afterschool activities. I gave her my proposal and told her that I would teach the class myself as a volunteer. That would at least eliminate one obstacle. All I needed was funding for the books and the materials required to teach the class. The Rotary Club agreed and so did the school! I was suddenly in a position to teach six of the 17 principles of success to eighteen fourth, fifth and sixth graders!

In preparation for the six-week program, I wrote an outline that was labeled a "pilot program." That was as close as I had come to writing the curriculum. At the conclusion of the six-weeks, I held a debrief meeting with the school counselor that assisted me with the class and the school principal. They had taken the time to discuss the program with each of the students and provided me with feedback. In turn, I was to write a report and provide it to the Rotary Club so that they could be confident that they had spent their money wisely.

The feedback I had received was largely positive. The kids referred to it as their "leadership" class and by all indications, they enjoyed our time together. However, I was told that I had attempted to cover too much material in too little time and, according to the counselor, I had not included enough interactive activities. I had done more "presenting" than I had "teaching." No kidding! Like I said, I was not a teacher! But this time the experience was more positive than negative and I was not willing to give up on the program because of *my* limitations. It was time to rethink my approach.

"Persistence, concentration of effort, and definiteness of purpose are major sources for achievement—each of which is impossible without *belief.*"

According to Napoleon Hill, the subconscious receives and files sense impressions or thoughts, regardless of their nature. The subconscious acts first on the dominating desires which have been mixed with emotional feelings, such as faith. The mixing of faith with a plan, or purpose, intended for submission to the subconscious mind, may be done only through the imagination. So I kept my options open and my antennas up.

At the beginning of the next school year, I was invited to become a mentor as part of the PACERS (Positive Achievement and Creativity Equals Righteous Success) Program. PACERS was named by the Rock Island, Illinois High School students it serves. It is an academically-based mentoring program designed to help under-performing students succeed and ultimately graduate from high school. PACERS provides an on-going intervention beginning with the freshman year and ending with high school graduation. It is designed to help students with personal, social and academic success.

The PACERS program is a partnership between the Rock Island High School and Western Illinois University (WIU) and is funded by a grant. The mentors are adults from the community who are paid a small monthly stipend which is part of the grant. Mentors meet with students at school in a classroom setting during the regular school day once per week. They also participate in a variety of community service activities with students. When not in school, mentors involve their students in a variety of activities left only to their imaginations. The goal of the program is to provide students with academic and personal support, and stability while building positive long-term relationships.

As of the 2010/2011 school year, there were approximately fifty-one students from the freshman, sophomore and junior classes and twenty-one mentors.

At the 2009 Christmas banquet, Dr. Holly Nikels, Associate Professor at WIU, and Grant Administrator for the PACERS program indicated that they were going to look at implementing some sort of curriculum into the program. The PACERS program had value, and they were realizing positive results, but they wanted more "meat" and simply teaching the students study skills was not enough. Whatever they did had to be fun and it had to be non-traditional. They did not want the PACERS program to become just another "class." They also wanted to provide the mentors more guidance as part of the new curriculum and help them become more actively involved in the program.

I could not *believe* what I was hearing! This was the exact opportunity that I was looking for, and I was ready to take full advantage of it!

Dr. Nikels and I met over coffee a few days later and I gave her my proposal. From there I met with the school counselors involved with the program and explained the program and its value to them. I also described how it could work within the classroom based on what I had learned from the counselor and the principal during my elementary school pilot program. They got excited! The next step was to get Judy Williamson involved. She needed to conduct the site-based certification training.

For the teachers and counselors to teach the principles in a classroom setting, they were required to have a site-based certification from the Napoleon Hill World Learning Center. The mentors were included in the training so that they bought into the program. It also gave them a better understanding of what the program was all about. Judy Williamson and Chino Martinez conducted the two-day training session and I assisted.

According to Napoleon Hill, no individual may have great power without availing himself of the "Master Mind." Mastermind is defined as "Coordination of knowledge and effort, in a spirit of harmony, between two or more people, for the attainment of a definite purpose." When two or more people coordinate in a spirit of harmony, and work toward a definite objective, they place themselves in position, through that alliance, to absorb power directly from the great universal storehouse of Infinite Intelligence. This is the greatest of all sources of power.

In his book, *Think and Grow Rich*, Mr. Hill teaches us that faith is the only known antidote for failure. It is the starting point for the accumulation of all riches. Whatever we convince our subconscious mind to *believe*, we will receive. We rise to high positions or remain at the bottom because of conditions we can control if we desire to control them. Each of us holds the power within. I was feeling the *power!* My *belief* was growing!

The feedback from the mentors following the training was fantastic! They were pumped about the upcoming school year. So were Dr. Nikels, the counselors and the teachers. They *all* saw the value of the program and were as convinced as I was that it would have a significant positive impact on the students.

I met with Dr. Nikels, the counselors and the teachers the week following the teacher/mentor training session to finalize our plans and approach for implementing the program. I would teach a second certification course for the mentors that were unable to attend the first more formal training. This training would be more of a program overview and include a brief introduction of the six principles that would be taught in the classroom. I would also teach the first student class. The purpose of this first class is to provide the students with some background about Napoleon Hill. I would also give them an overview of the program and the six principles being taught over the course of the upcoming school year. The actual in-school classes will be taught by the newly certified counselors and teachers. Mentors and students alike will participate in the weekly classes. The program will focus on six of the seventeen principles, the same six I taught during the pilot program at the elementary school. The big difference here is that we will take up to four weeks to learn each principle. As to the curriculum, a formal one still does not exist. However, I have created outlines that include each of the principles, a list of the concepts that support each principle, and the terms and definitions used to describe each principle. The counselors are going to come up with a list of activities to make the learning experience more interactive and fun. They will also write the curriculum and I will participate in that process. I will also be teaching a quarterly "Lunch & Learn" for the mentors, the counselors, and the teachers. The goal will be to address any challenges they have with the program, brainstorm ideas for improvement, find out how the students are handling the information, and to cover the next principle being taught.

Napoleon Hill says, "Your *belief*, or faith, is the element which determines the action of your subconscious mind." The subconscious mind will translate a thought driven by fear into reality just as readily as it will translate a thought driven by courage or faith into reality.

"It is a well-known fact," he writes, "that one comes, finally to believe whatever one repeats to one's self. If you fill your mind with fear, doubt and unbelief in your ability to connect with and use the forces of Infinite Intelligence, the law of auto-suggestion will take this spirit of unbelief and use it as a pattern by which your subconscious mind will translate it into its physical equivalent."

Faith removes all limitations. I am beginning to feel the power that faith provides.

I had an idea supported by an action plan. While I did not devote every waking moment to the pursuit of my goal, I was prepared and open to receive whatever was sent to me by the Universe. That belief allowed me to further my goal and help me move closer to fulfilling my purpose. However, this story is far from finished. My journey includes many miles not yet covered, but the journey has begun and begun in earnest.

In his book, Think and Grow Rich, *Napoleon Hill teaches us that belief does not come easily nor does it happen overnight. The subconscious mind takes any orders given it in a spirit of absolute faith (belief), and acts upon those orders, although the orders often have to be presented over and over again, through repetition, before they are interpreted by the subconscious mind. I continually repeat my goals and I continually struggle to* always *believe.*

The afterschool program I originally envisioned would target elementary school students is now being taught to high school students as part of their regular school day. While the class is limited to only fifty-one students, they include students from the new incoming freshman class to the new sophomore and junior classes. This small group of students will receive between two and four years of Napoleon Hill teaching during their regular school day, one day per week for the remainder of their high school careers. In addition, their mentors will participate in the training and together, multiple Mastermind groups will be formed. In addition, other people with expertise in curriculum development will now be working with me to formalize the program being developed. We will have input from the students receiving the training and from the mentors supporting and encouraging their students to pursue their dreams regardless of their past, current or future circumstances. The program is fully funded and has the support of two noteworthy educational institutions. We are definitely moving in the right direction!

Faith, the confident *belief* in the truth, is truly the basis for all miracles. *Belief* is *my* secret. It is persistent and consistent faith in action!

About Gail Brooks

Gail Brooks is a public relations consultant for public housing authorities nationally. She also owns a business development company that is dedicated to helping people establish their own businesses allowing them to generate a secondary income stream. Gail is a certified instructor for the Napoleon Hill World Learning Center and has been instrumental in establishing the Napoleon Hill "Reach for Success" program for children. gailbrooks1@hotmail.com

9

The "Secret" Is No Secret At All!

by Phil Barlow

WHITE, GEORGIA

One Friday afternoon thirty years ago, I was sitting in an airport waiting for a connecting flight. It was long before cell phones and laptop computers were available and to pass the time I was enjoying a session of people watching. You can tell a lot about someone just by watching them walk through an airport. The smile or frown on their face, the way they hold their body, the pace in which they walk, the way they are dressed and many other traits are telling signs.

As I was panning the crowd, I glanced at the table beside me and noticed an old used and abused paperback copy of Napoleon Hill's classic book, *Think and Grow Rich*. I had never heard of Napoleon Hill or his book, however at that time in my life, I was searching for some answers. I was among the ranks of the uninspired and hoping, that one day, my ship would come in.

Call it luck, coincidence or even fate. I don't know what to call it; however I do know finding and reading Hill's book changed my life. I read just enough that afternoon to know

I wanted to learn more about Napoleon Hill and his success philosophy.

The very next day, after returning home, I bought a copy of the book and read it for the first time. In the intervening years, I have re-read the book several times and there has been no limit to the number of times I have referenced specific material from it. I consider it to be one of the best investments I have ever made.

During my early readings I found myself spending an inordinate amount of time searching for the "Secret." After all, Napoleon Hill himself clearly stated that readers will have an opportunity to recognize the Carnegie secret at least once in every chapter and that it is mentioned no fewer than one hundred times throughout the book. Well who am I to question the man who dedicated over twenty years of his life assimilating and organizing the material referenced in *Think and Grow Rich.*

As time passed and I became a student of Napoleon Hill's philosophy, my perspective on the idea of a miraculous "secret" changed. Rather than looking outside my own boundaries in search for the answer I re-focused my efforts on my own observations and experiences and then compared them to the conclusions Hill derived from his research. Learning from a well documented philosophy can be very valuable and at the same time it's important to recognize that, from time to time, even the wisest philosophers have done nothing more than guess about their conclusions.

When I began my search for the truth, at least what was true for me, I took a hard look at the world around me. I paid particular attention to what was working and what wasn't; which friends and acquaintances we're doing well and which ones were not; which kids did well in school and athletics and which ones struggled; which families appeared to be loving and caring and which ones appeared to be dysfunctional.

Whether reading Hill's works or doing my own personal research, I constantly looked for the elusive "secret." After thirty years I still haven't found it. Although I haven't found a secret, I have benefited from the digging and searching. It has been almost like digging for gold and finding a diamond. I haven't found the gold, but I have found what has turned out to be very valuable and beneficial to me. The light of understanding has been shining bright for me for a very long time.

I have found no "secrets"; just natural laws and simple lessons that are time tested and proven without a shadow of a doubt. I have built a life based on these lessons and have grown and achieved levels of success well beyond anything I could have imagined in my earlier years.

Who knows, maybe this is exactly what Napoleon Hill had in mind when he suggested to his readers and students that there is a secret to be found to those who are ready and searching for it. That approach certainly produces a motive . . . a strong motive. Hill was very direct when he stated that all individual achievements are the result of a motive or a combination of motives.

Could it be that all he wanted to do was create a motive and ignite a fire of intense desire under his readers?

OK . . . no secret for me. There were, however, revelations; "Ah-ha" moments when the light came on. Why? What caused this to happen?

As I read, studied and observed, I noticed there were simple truths that made a lot of sense to me. The first thing that got my attention was Hill's position on how the mind works and how the power of the mind is universal, available to the humblest person as it is to the greatest. And, that greatness comes from the ability to recognize the power of the mind, embrace it and use it.

The concept that everyone has the potential of tapping into the power of the mind resonated with me. When I repeated out loud and with feeling the statement: Whatever the mind can conceive and believe, it can achieve, I felt incredible energy. Powerful, very powerful words: Conceive, Believe, Achieve.

The next thing that got my attention was that everything that is created begins in the form of a thought impulse. Nothing can be created that is not first conceived in thought. For me, that was great news because I learned and believed the power of thought is the only thing over which any human being has complete, unquestionable control. We are the only creatures on earth with the power of self-determination and the right to choose what our thoughts and actions will be.

I also learned all great things come from ideas. Where do ideas come from? Our thoughts, our mind, our imagination!

I rationalized my way through these truths about thoughts and ideas and came to the realization that all achievements, all earned riches, have their beginning in an idea. We are where we are because of the dominating thoughts we permit to occupy our minds. Is this a secret? I don't think so. Psychologists have known this truth for a very long time. That being the case, why don't more people have an understanding about this? It's a shame that so many people are drifting and floundering when these truths are readily available to everyone.

Why do so many people ignore the power of their own minds? Why do they go with the flow; whatever comes along. . . . good or bad? It's evident to anyone who can see beyond the tip of their nose, one of the biggest tragedies that exist in the world today is how many people are drifting aimlessly through life with no sense of direction at all.

It seems so simple, but it's true. We have total control of our thoughts. We have the power of choice, yet so many choose to live a life of hopelessness.

It doesn't have to be that way. As a matter of fact, it shouldn't be that way. Living a life with no purpose and no sense of direction is in direct conflict with Nature's design. Nature gives us a set of tools and rewards us in a big way if we use them. At the same time, she will penalize us beyond compare if we don't accept and use them.

The truth is there is no such thing as SOMETHING FOR NOTHING. Success and achievement cannot be had without paying a price. Those who are not intentionally searching for success cannot have it at any price.

"Ah—Ha"!!!!!!!!!

You mean you have to take ownership of your life? You have to pay a price and there are no free lunches? We'll that's a novel position, especially considering the entitlement mentality that exists with so many people around the world today. This isn't a new phenomenon. It's been this way since the beginning of time. Some people excel. Some don't. Some people are willing to go the extra mile; others do just enough to get by. Some people know where they are going before they go. Some people drift in the direction of the prevailing wind.

In *Think and Grow Rich*, Napoleon Hill stated that all achievement, all earned riches, have their beginning in an idea. I've already touched on that. He goes on to state that if you are ready, you already possess half of what you need by understanding the power of your mind and how thoughts work. I believe the other half has a lot to do with why we are here on this planet. I believe we are here for a specific purpose, a reason for being. We're here on this earth for a very short time and it's a great shame that so many people drift and coast their lives away, without having a clue why they are here.

The first thing that has to be done to transform thoughts into reality is to have a clearly conceived idea of what it is that you wish to achieve. A "Definite Purpose," something definite and specific. It helps to know where you're going before you go.

What a different story the "drifters" in life would have to tell if only they would adopt a definite purpose, and stand by that purpose until it had time to become an all-consuming obsession.

In my youth and as a young adult I believed hard work, Going the Extra Mile, would take me anywhere I wanted to go. My parents taught me well and in my early years, because I was willing to work harder than most others, I achieved a moderate level of success. Granted, I was doing OK but the problem was I wasn't definite about what I was doing. I was taking the proverbial "shotgun" approach hoping that something would hit the target.

The light finally came on for me when I accepted the absolute need to establish a Definite Major Purpose for my life, a plan of action for its attainment and a burning desire to possess it.

It's not too important for your plan to be sound. If you find that it's not sound, change it, modify it, get it right. It is very important that you are definite about what you are going after. Your purpose is your reason for being. I don't think this is a secret, however I do believe it is a fundamental truth that can and will have a profound and lasting "positive" impact on a person's life.

If the thing you wish to do is right, and you believe in it, go for it with all the gusto you can muster up! All achievements, no matter what their nature or purpose, must begin with an intense burning desire for something definite. Find something you love to do and then love to do it!

As soon as you have decided on your Definite Major Purpose, you can expect to enjoy some immediate advantages. You will find it to be amazing just how fast these things will occur. Having a definite purpose will ensure you develop self-reliance, personal initiative, imagination, enthusiasm, self-discipline and concentration of effort. All of these things are of vital importance to success.

You will develop a level of specialization, not previously held. You will become proficient in budgeting time and money. Your mind will automatically be in tune to opportunities. You will be inspired to act with courage. You will develop the capacity to reach decisions. You will inspire others to cooperate with you. Your mind will open and be receptive to faith and you will become obsessed with succeeding not failing.

This is a powerful start, but it's only the beginning.

Each of us is what we are because of the dominating thoughts we permit to occupy our minds. We have the power of choice. Somewhere in our make-up, possibly the cells of our brain, lies sleeping the seed of achievement. When aroused and put into action, the seed will carry you to heights well beyond your current state.

Think and Grow Rich is the perfect book to introduce people to the ideas and concepts developed as a result of Napoleon Hill's extensive work. It is a quick, easy and enticing read and gets the creative juices flowing. His other works may have been a little too in-depth to attract the masses. He created a strong motive when he introduced the idea of a "secret" answer. It certainly sinks the hook in and causes people to want to search and learn more. *Think and Grow Rich* is a spring board and can be used as a segue to even greater insight.

For those who want to better understand the power of the mind and how to effectively utilize the natural success system that exists in each and every one of us, you should commit to studying and learning the 17 principles of success outlined in Napoleon Hill's "Law of Success" or one of the programs offered by the Napoleon Hill World Learning Center. The answers, in my opinion, are not in the elusive "secret." They can be found in the extensive study material published by Napoleon Hill over 80 years ago.

Learn how to recognize the power of your own mind, embrace it and use it. Be persistent, concentrate your effort and become obsessed with your definiteness of purpose. If you're willing to pay the price, there is no doubt good things will result for you!

About Phil Barlow

Phil Barlow began his career as a teacher, administrator and coach. For over three decades he has held numerous sales, marketing and leadership positions. Currently, he is a Vice President of the leading carpet manufacturer in the world. Phil is also a certified leader for the Napoleon Hill Foundation. He can be reached at: phil.barlow@shawinc.com.

10

Success is Possible by Tapping Infinate Intelligence

by Carlos Quesada
SAN JOSE, COSTA RICA

In 1970, at the age of 22, I got married. By 1974 I had a daughter, we had lost a baby, and my wife was pregnant again. I was already struggling financially when my father suffered a stroke, putting me in charge of his urban transport company. He had just purchased five new buses using his house as collateral. At the same time, my younger brother and sister were still in school, which I was now obliged to pay for.

I decided then to abandon my own college studies in order to deal with my family situation.

One day I was in a bookstore when the title *Think and Grow Rich* caught my eye. I bought the book (and still treasure that copy) but I must admit that upon first reading it, it had no effect whatsoever on me. To paraphrase Dr. Hill, I was not ready to receive the wisdom and advice.

Shortly thereafter, I was in the same bookstore and discovered *Positive Mental Attitude: A Road to Success*, by Hill and W. Clement Stone. Reading this book led me to study the philosophy of *Think and Grow Rich* more carefully, and then, as if being touched with a magic wand, I discovered the secret that would help me achieve success. It was a mind-blowing experience.

I do not want to reveal the secret here, partly because I think it is a little different for each person. Discovering the secret for yourself, as Dr. Hill says, results in much deeper comprehension. However, I know from experience that applying Hill's and Stone's teachings result in success in all parts of life, personal, familial, financial, spiritual, and ethical.

For nearly 40 years these two books have been on my bedside table, and I consult them daily, always taking notes, highlighting, and underlining passages. I always find something new to use and apply to my life. It is incredible how every time I read the books I can find different combinations and connections that will benefit not only me but also those around me.

I set forth in life in a different way than others because I communicated with Infinite Intelligence. Using the principles of success and the power of prayer and faith, the problems I faced in the 1970s and 80s were overcome. In 1982 an opportunity arrived just as Dr. Hill had said it would, on the sly through the back door, and my company was offered the representation of Spanish truck brand Pegaso in Costa Rica. This opportunity changed my business and also changed me personally, as constant travelling to Europe broadened my horizons and gave me a new appreciation for our world.

Eventually the application of the 13 steps in *Think and Grow Rich* with the 17 principles taught in *Positive Mental Attitude* allowed me to build 6 companies that employ 350 persons and give a dignified standard of living to more than 1,500. I enjoy professional relationships with collaborators in several disciplines as we meet to apply the Mastermind Principle.

At home my work toward my Definite Major Purpose has led to a priceless relationship with my wife, three incredible daughters, and four grandchildren. We share together the philosophy of success and continue to grow personally, financially, and spiritually. I am also blessed with my father and mother who at 94 and 84 years old, respectively, both enjoy excellent health.

My plan for success has always started with the phrase, "Do it now." I added a few more words, with all due respect to Dr. Hill and Mr. Stone: "Do it now, do it right away: be practical, logical, and simple." The shortest distance between two points is a straight line, and I always seek to use the direct path to finish quicker and be more effective.

Over time, applying the success principles and the power of Infinite Intelligence, I developed my own self-motivational slogan: "Not just efficiency and efficacy, but above all, effectiveness." I urge you to look up the word effectiveness in the dictionary yourself. Doing that will make the definition even more meaningful to you. You can have efficiency and efficacy yet lack effectiveness; likewise you can be effective with little or no efficiency or efficacy. I want you to learn where our word effectiveness comes from and how we have it always.

I owe everything to the secret that came to me through the books I read and the actions I applied. I found it, and you can too, if you will realize you are the most important person in your life, that thought must be followed by *immediate action,* and believe with utmost faith that "whatever the mind can conceive and believe, the mind can achieve."

About Carlos Quesada

Carlos A. Quesada was born in San Jose, Costa Rica in September of 1947. Actually he is the owner of companies dedicated to the service of urban transportation for passengers, trucks and machinery sales, spare part sales for automotive vehicles, inversions and financial activities.

Éxito, Es Posible Comulgue Con La Inteligencia Infinita

Por Carlos Quesada

SAN JOSÉ, COSTA RICA

Me casé muy joven, en 1970 a la edad de 22 años. En el año 1974, ya tenía una hija, habíamos perdido un bebé y mi esposa estaba nuevamente embarazada.

Tenía en ese entonces serios problemas financieros, económicos y de otro tipo, incluyendo el hecho de que mi padre había sufrido un derrame cerebral y tuve que hacerme cargo desde ese momento de una empresa de transporte urbano con 5 buses recién adquiridos y garantizados con la casa de mis padres, todo estaba hipotecado y a punto de perderse. A su vez, se sumaba la situación de que mi hermano y mi hermana, menores que yo, aún estaban estudiando, lo cual también enfrenté de lleno.

Decidí, entonces, abandonar los estudios universitarios y hacerle frente a la situación familiar.

Buscando soluciones, un día, en una librería, me encontré de frente con el libro del señor Napoleón Hill "Piense y

Hágase Rico" (Editorial Bruguera Barcelona España, Cuarta Edición Diciembre 1974, Edición en lengua original Napoleon Hill 1966, Traducción J Piñeira 1972), cuyo título llamó mi atención y decidí adquirirlo.

Debo manifestar que la primera lectura del libro (que aún conservo como un gran tesoro) no surtió efecto alguno en mí (probablemente porque en ese momento no estaba en sintonía).

Pasando por la misma librería, poco tiempo después me encontré otro libro del señor Napoleón Hill, el cual había escrito junto al señor W. Clement Stone, titulado "Actitud Mental Positiva Un Camino Al Éxito". (Editorial Grijaldo, Barcelona, Publicación 1977.)

Combiné la lectura de ambos libros y los estudié a fondo y como tocado por una varita descubrí el secreto que luego emplearía para tener éxito. Fue como haber recibido un buen golpe mental y psicológico a la vez.

No voy aquí a revelarlo, ya que el secreto es diferente para cada persona, pero sé que aplicando lo explicado por el señor Napoleón Hill en el libro "Piense y Hágase Rico" y lo explicado por los señores Hill y Stone en el libro "Actitud Mental Positiva" se puede tener éxito en la vida en todos los órdenes: financieros, espirituales, ético, familiares. Además, como lo dice el señor Hill, la persona lo debe descubrir por sí mismo (kilómetro extra). Es más sólida entonces su comprensión.

A partir de entonces y durante estos casi 40 años estos dos libros han estado siempre en la cabecera de mi mesa de noche y los consulto a día a día, estudiando un capítulo casi a diario, anotando, marcando y subrayando. Siempre encuentro algo nuevo para usar y aplicar en mis actividades. Es increíble como se encuentran cada vez, diferentes combinaciones, para aplicarlas en beneficio individual y colectivo.

Partí hacia delante, de una forma diferente a como creo parten todos los demás, ya que me puse en comunicación con la Inteligencia Infinita para que a través de dicho Ente Abstracto se iluminara el camino y me guiara en la aplicación de los 13 pasos de "Piense y Hágase Rico" y de los 17 principios de "Actitud Mental Positiva Un Camino Al Éxito", empleando el poder de la oración y la fe absoluta.

La aplicación de los 13 pasos y de los 17 principios me permitieron salir de los problemas (¡qué gran bendición tener problemas!) que en esa década de los años 70 y 80 tenía.

En el año 1982, sorpresivamente y de forma insospechada y "socarrona", la oportunidad llegó por la puerta trasera, con una oferta de representación de camiones españoles, marca Pegaso para Costa Rica, que nos cambió a todos notablemente la vida a partir de ese momento. Con eso llegaron también viajes constantes a Europa que cambiaron la visión panorámica del mundo y me ampliaron el horizonte.

La aplicación de los 13 pasos, de los 17 principios, basado en la comunicación con la Inteligencia Infinita y siguiendo el esfuerzo del kilómetro extra, me permitió crear seis empresas que le dan trabajo directo a 350 personas, colaboradores en diferentes disciplinas a los cuales acudo para el consejo especializado en reuniones que tenemos regularmente aplicando el principio de la "Mente Maestra", dándoles vida digna a más de 1500, más todas las demás personas de las industrias auxiliares que ayudan a seguir adelante a las empresas.

La aplicación del plan que puse en acción me permitió crear una familia con una esposa que no tiene precio y tres hijas increíbles (ahora hay 4 nietos que son una bendición) que comparten a nivel familiar la filosofía tanto del señor Hill como del señor Stone para seguir creciendo espiritualmente, personalmente, financieramente, éticamente, materialmente.

También cuento con la bendición de que, actualmente, mi padre tiene 94 años y mi madre tiene 84 años de edad, y ambos gozan de excelente salud.

Desde el primer momento puse el plan en acción "Hágalo ahora", al que sí le agregué con respeto a los señores Hill y Stone de "Hágalo ahora, hágalo ya: práctico, lógico y sencillo". La distancia más corta entre dos puntos es la línea recta y apliqué el atajo de la línea recta para llegar más rápido, terminar más rápido y tener efectividad más rápido.

Aplicando el poder de la Inteligencia Infinita con el poder de la oración llegué a diseñar un slogan de automotivación para tener éxito en todos los órdenes de la vida: no sólo con eficiencia y eficacia, sino sobre todo con efectividad.

Se puede tener eficiencia y eficacia y no conseguir nada efectividad; y se puede tener efectividad con poco o ninguna eficiencia y eficacia. Ruego con respeto buscar en el diccionario la palabra efectividad: de dónde viene y cómo la llevamos siempre. No quiero descubrirla aquí. Quiero que cada quien lo haga por sí mismo, mediante el kilómetro extra.

Todo lo debo a que el secreto llegó a mí a través de la parte del libro dedicada a la Inteligencia Infinita, la cual uní con la parte positiva y práctica del señor Stone, aplicando fe, poder de la oración, compartir con los demás, ayudar, servir.

Encontré la llave que cualquier persona puede encontrar a través de estos dos libros, sobre todo "Piense y Hágase Rico", en sus 13 pasos, sabiendo que todo lo que usted logre, es porque usted es la persona más importante y puede conseguir lo que se proponga en la vida, mediante el pensamiento seguido de acción inmediata, póngase en movimiento inmediatamente y creyendo con fe que:

"Lo que la mente pueda concebir se puede crear y lograr".

Carlos A. Quesada

Carlos A. Quesada nació en San José, Costa Rica en septiembre de 1947. Actualmente es dueño de empresas dedicadas al servicio de transporte urbano de pasajeros, venta de camiones y maquinaria, venta de repuestos para vehículos automotores, inversiones y actividades financieras.

The secret to which I refer has been mentioned no fewer than a hundred times throughout this book. It has not been directly named, for it seems to work more successfully when it is merely uncovered and left in sight, where those who are ready and searching for it, may pick it up.

–NAPOLEON HILL

11

How to Master the Psychology of the Secret: The Secret to The Secret

by Thomas M. Brown, Psy. D.
OREM, UTAH

In this chapter, I will present what I believe to be Hill's secret that he alluded to in his book, *Think and Grow Rich*. I want to go beyond just discussing what I believe this secret to be. My desire is to take you into the realm to where you can actually achieve the concrete application of this secret through specific, step-by-step instructions I have learned by applying modern-day tangible, sequenced processes, strategies, methods, techniques, and skills that are based on my professional training and personal research. I have mentioned other material that I have found helpful. Also, I have included educational lineage to give credit from whom I learned and to provide contextual background with the hope of promoting a better understanding upon which my conclusions and ideas are based.

To provide context, as of August 2010, I have been reading books composed or inspired by Napoleon Hill for approximately ten years. I am a licensed psychologist in the States of Utah and Iowa. I live in the United States of America and have a practice in Utah. I have a Doctorate of Psychology (Psy. D.). I have also studied a way by which this sixth sense (Hill dedicated a chapter to this sixth sense in *Think and Grow Rich*) can be turned on or off at will and cultivated as early as childhood.

Because I receive deep joy helping others, when I design seminars, my goal is to give people powerful skills, strategies, methods, techniques, and processes they can use the same day they learn them. As I have read and listened to Hill's materials, I have thought about how to apply what I know to increase my and others' success with and access to this secret. I will condense my training and research into ideas, concepts, and activities that you could do with the goal of implementing this secret.

First, I believe the secret is this process: "To take control and possession of one's own mind and direct it to the objective of one's own choosing." To do this, one must have the means by which to control one's mind and then sustain focus on one's objective. One must also be able to know what one wants and clearly articulate it. Next, let us examine some of Napoleon Hill's methods by which one could do this process before examining other such methods. In his works, he outlines basic motives and the importance of associating your goals or Definite Chief Aim to as many of those basic motives as possible. He also discussed in his works the stimulants of the mind. He also discussed how to eliminate the basic fears. With certainty, it would be logical to conclude that by associating one's goals or aim with basic motive or mind stimulant and by eliminating fears, one's mind would be more controllable and directible! Now, how might we accomplish this? Let us begin by identifying the motives, stimulants, and fears.

Hill also listed nine basic motives, which included: hope, love, revenge, sex, intoxication, self-preservation, fear, freedom (of body and mind), and life after death. As further comment, I believe this idea of life after death can include such desires as the wish to go to heaven. I also believe this idea of life after death could include having a foundation, organization, educational fund, or building named after oneself.

The stimulants of the mind (p. 184) that he listed included: desire for sex expression; love; desire for fame, power, financial gain, or money; music; friendship; master mind alliance; mutual suffering; auto-suggestion; fear; narcotics (e.g., intoxicating substances); and alcohol. In examining these lists of basic motives and mind stimulant, you will notice overlapping items, such as love.

Hill also listed basic fears (p. 228) including: old age, ill health, poverty, criticism, loss of love, and death. I would add two others to the list, which I think Hill alluded to in some of his works. One such fear would be the fear of the unknown. The other would be one's own personal fear or fears, which I think we all have. Based on your own background, culture, experiences, family history, temperament, and so forth, you have your own set of fears that are unique to you. May I direct you to page 250 in *Think and Grow Rich*, 1937 edition, to begin to read about what Hill may have thought to be a very important set of solutions to conquer fears!

Now, having identified the basic motives, mind stimulants, and basic fears, let us now discover methods by which Hill recommended we control and direct our minds. One method Hill discussed was autosuggestion. Simply by repeating one's goal or aim to oneself before going to sleep or as one was rising in after slumber was a form of autosuggestion Hill mentioned in his works. Repeating the goal or objective multiple times a day would be another application. Repetition can definitely help one learn new skills. Repetition helps develop habits of thought, behavior, AND feeling! I believe repetition in and of itself tells the subconscious and/or unconscious mind that something is important. On page 57, he recommended we commit it to memory, as well.

Suggestions may be more influential when emotionalized by love or faith. I have discovered in both a personal and professional capacity that adding emotion to thoughts and activities can be quintessential to motivation and success. Hill discussed emotionalizing thoughts and objectives with stimulants of the mind and the basic motives.

On page 52, Hill writes: "The emotions of faith, love, and sex are the most powerful of all the major positive emotions." In other areas, Hill talked about the basic motives and suggested connecting as many of the basic motives as possible to one's goals or aim. Self-preservation could also be added to this list of motives to which one could connect one's goals or aim. . . . After all, if you are convinced your life depends on completing a goal, how much more motivated might you be to complete it quickly?

Hill dedicated a whole chapter to faith. I will also provide methods to increase your faith. Faith in what? We will address that, too!

Hill discussed also how creative imagination was important in success. I believe this too could be a form of autosuggestion, as he states on page 71: "auto suggestion is a term which applies to all suggestions and self-administered stimuli which reach one's mind through the five senses." Though creative imagination might be a more complicated process and more vivid and activating than simply reading a sentence to oneself, I still consider it thought, for reasons I hope will become more clear and understandable as you continue reading.

As another form of controlling one's mind, Hill encouraged people to imagine themselves as having completed their goals and aims as concretely and emotionally as possible. As an example with money, on page 36: "see and feel and believe yourself already in possession of the money."

In one of his works, Hill described a positive mental attitude (PMA) as being one of the important riches in life. If you were to have more PMA, this could lead to more control of your mind that you may keep yourself more focused on your goals or aim. (In terms of Hill's work, I would place a positive mental attitude in the arena of interpretation and his concept of self-confidence in the arena of meaning. The ideas of interpretation and meaning will be addressed later in this chapter.)

I believe the development of the sixth sense to be an important part of developing this secret for yourself. "The sixth sense in not something you can turn on and off at will. Ability to use this great power comes slowly, through application of other principles outlined in this book. Seldom does an individual come into workable knowledge of the sixth sense before the age of forty. More often the knowledge is not available until one is well past fifty, and this, for the reason that spiritual forces, with which the sixth sense is so closely related, do not mature and become usable except through years of meditation, self-examination, and serious though." (p. 225) Although this may have been true at the time Hill wrote this manuscript, I believe it is now possible to train oneself to develop and apply the sixth sense at will. I will comment later in this chapter why this new process I learned makes the use of this sixth sense an activity that can be learned and applied at will, even at the age of childhood.

Now that we have identified areas and foci to increase control of your mind, let us cover specific methods by which people have liberated themselves from fears and increased their desire and motivation for productive, constructive goal-oriented behavior.

I also believe Hill discussed another method in his materials by which one could gain greater control over one's mind. He presents methods by which he used his imagination to help keep his mind focused on his objectives. I believe he referred to one group as the 10 guardians or princes, which included love, romance, hope, faith, sound physical health, material wealth, patience, wisdom, peace of mind, and Normhill. He also discussed his invisible counselor meetings, in which he discussed imagining himself at a table, presiding over a meeting of those whom he wished to seek advise and/or emulate their desired personal characteristics (see pages 218 to 224).

Let us now cover one more method that Hill addressed. Another method for furthering your goals or Definite Chief Aim is to write down an objective before going to sleep. I know a mentor of mine, Dave Dobson, Ph.D., has recommended this and if my memory serves me correct, Hill has in an audio program. It is my understanding that the reasoning behind this is that the subconscious section of the mind takes it inside itself and works on it during sleep. I have found this to be helpful when I use it regularly, and synchronicities appear to increase in my life.

Now, as we go deeper still, I would request you direct your attention to a perhaps more expansive and inclusive view of thought with the hope we can understand and intervene with this process. As a result of my education and experiences (both personal and professional), I have concluded that there are a number of features and facets to this concept of thought. Perhaps at its simplest level, a thought could be construed as a phrase or sentence within one's head consisting of a noun and verb. Attitudes or beliefs might be conceptualized as a series of interconnected or associated thoughts. Some people might think more in images, pictures, montages, or movies rather than words, phrases, or sentences. Still, I would classify such visuals as thoughts. On page 19, Hill states that "thoughts are things." He stated: "our brains become magnetized with the dominating thoughts." (p. 29) Although we cannot ask Hill what his idea of "thoughts" might have been, we can notice in his materials that he refers to imagination, autosuggestions, and beliefs all as mental processes by which we can change our thinking and character.

Also, our thoughts can be what we say to ourselves and the tones of voice with which we think or talk to ourselves can influence our emotional states. This idea I discovered as a direct result of having studied Neuro-Linguistic Programming (NLP), in which the founders discuss submodalities. (NLP will be addressed later in this chapter.) Think about thinking to yourself the question: "How am I going to do this?" Now, if you think this question to yourself with an inner voice that is calm, collected, and confident you will likely have a much different feeling than if you think this question to yourself with an inner voice that is panicked, insecure, and hopeless. This is how the tone and perhaps volume of our inner voice can impact how we feel. Controlling the tone and volume of this inner voice will likely impact our self-confidence and character. Indeed, I believe to have this quality of self-confidence (which Hill described as being imperative; see pages 57 to 58) we must speak to ourselves with an inner voice that is both confident and positive.

What methods, strategies, process, techniques, and skills can be used to change our thinking and feelings? I would describe feelings as the progeny of thoughts. The field of cognitive psycho-therapy encourages people to change their thinking to change how they feel. Indeed, Hill writes about the importance of "changing one's thoughts" to help one feel more positive (p. 198). From the field of cognitive psychotherapy, the list of people who have developed or pioneered work in this regard include: Jeffrey Young, Ph.D.; Albert Ellis, Ph.D.; Aaron Beck, M.D.; Judith Beck, Ph.D.; Marsha Linehan, Ph.D., ABPP; David Burns, M.D. This list is by no means exhaustive, but I do want to credit those from whom I learned. Books by these authors contain specific processes by which one can change one's own thoughts. Rather than recommending a specific book by any of these authors, I would encourage you to look in a book store (online or in an actual building) and decide for yourself which one might best suit you. I have been partial to Young, Ellis, and Burns.

I believe there is also a process by which thoughts interact and build upon each other. I remember learning about this hypothetical process in graduate school, but do not remember which class or who proposed this process. I will do my best to explain this model to you to the best of my ability from memory.

This process presents how a person might develop conclusions (or emotional reaction) about a situation, idea, person, place, thing, or event based on a concatenation beginning at sensory perception and terminating at the conclusion (or emotional reaction). The first process of this model is attention. As we move through the world, we have chances to pay attention. We can pay attention with our senses. We can pay attention to certain senses. We can pay attention to certain aspects of our environment and not others. Then, depending to what we might attend, we can give the input an interpretation. The interpretation may be to classify the input (the sensory input upon which we attend) as constructive or destructive to our well-being, safety, goals, and so forth. After providing an interpretation to ourselves, we can assign this interpretation a meaning. This meaning we give it will likely be influenced by our ideas regarding our identity (who we think we are), degree of control (over what we perceive), and abilities (or skills). The implication is that even if the interpretation is negative, if we have faith in our ability to cope, our emotion response (the conclusion) will likely be more positive than if we do not have faith in our abilities.

Indeed, in one of his books, Hill dedicated an entire chapter to attention management. (I believe the title was called Concentration.) Our next topic leads in to the development of the sixth sense as an attention management strategy. I learned methods taught to the military remote viewing team. With this highly structured process I learned I can direct my mind to explore any topic of my choosing. Discovering my optimum trajectory or my optimum remote viewing target have been two very rewarding projects. I have helped in missing person cases. Some people chose this remote viewing process to find a vocation or mate. Others have used this to answer questions or mysteries of life. You do not leave your body or close your eyes to do this. You are very alert and focused during this entire process, lucid about what you want and what you are doing. That is why one of my mentors has called this an attention management strategy.

Since learning this process, I am convinced that this sixth sense Hill discussed in *Think and Grow Rich* is capable of being cultivated, controlled, and taught. Gone is the need to wait for age forty. Gone is the need to wait for it to inform you at its choosing. Now, you can command it to provide you the information you need. For one mentor, I attended three of his workshops: advanced skills, capstone, and professional course. (I believe he advertised the professional course as being offered one time only—and never to be offered again.)

Let us now direct our attention upon methods by which I have decreased my fears. I am convinced a healthy body is more likely to lead to a healthy mind. It appears Hill strongly believed in cultivating health. "No person may enjoy outstanding success without good health." (p. 128) I have researched and/or on my own experienced how physical exercise can help in reducing anxieties, improving mood, and expanding a sense of well-being. Diet has also helped me. For example, when I use my juicer, I tend to feel a greater sense of well-being. I have discovered it helpful to start my day before the sun rises, as well as spending time outside, either in direct or indirect natural sunlight, for about 30 minutes before 11:00 am.

For specific methods to intervene with one's mind to reduce fear and increase self-confidence, motivation, and desire, I would like to direct your attention now to my lineage with Dave Dobson. I went to meet him at his home on the San Juan Islands. I studied with him on several occasions and attended one of his seminars. I think of Dobson as one of the grandfathers of Neuro-Linguistic Programming.

To the best of my knowledge, Neuro-Linguistic Programming (NLP) began with Richard Bandler and John Grinder studying Milton Erickson, MD; Fritz Perls, MD; and Virginia Satir, Ph. D. to develop ideas and methods for change. But from what I understand Bandler and Grinder also studied Dobson. Dobson told me people would ask him: "When did you study under Erickson?" To the best of my knowledge,

Dobson did not study under Erickson. Apparently Erickson and Dobson developed similar methods independent of each other.

If Bandler and Grinder were the fathers of NLP, Dobson might be considered one of the grandfathers of NLP. I felt truly honored to have studied with him when he was alive. He taught me methods I have not seen or read anywhere else. I have used such methods to help myself and other people.

One of the most useful methods he taught me was having an objective, and then focusing on that objective. The idea being that objective would naturally guide your behavior effectively to your desired outcome. Focusing on an objective is another method by which one can take control of one's mind. Another process by which I help take control of my mind is through the Beach. I have found Dobson's Beach CD or tape to be very helpful with this. If you do decide to get his CD called Beach, remember to ask for the booklet that goes with it.

I think another important process to help direct the mind to ends of one's own choosing is becoming aware of what forces are guiding and shaping our decisions. As a specific area in which I have seen a number of people process is this area of trying to please and satisfy parents. Some people who have presented to my office are still trying to please their parents, living their lives with the hopes of achieving their approval. I feel sad when I see people well past 20 still living in this manner. Even more sad for me is when I see this in people who are well past 40 and/or have deceased parents. Why is it when we are mature, fully functioning adults, we still can feel we are in the shadows of our parents, with our parents' hopes, dreams, desires, and wants for us overshadowing our own directives? It is only possible to take possession of one's mind and direct it to ends of one's own choosing if this choice is independent of the desire for approval of others. (Remember the basic fears of criticism and loss of love?)

Another method I have used to integrate Hill's teachings in my life is from the field of hypnosis. Some people call this object symbol fractionation. Some people have called this a "forbidden technique." Again, I did not invent this process. I learned it at a seminar. I find it helps to have someone read the instructions to you and take notes when you are in a relaxed state of mind. You could do this yourself by reading the directions into a recording device and playing it back while you are in a relaxed state and having another recording device recording your responses to the objectives and questions.

The basic process is as follows: get comfortable. Turn the phone to the off position. Lock your door. Tell other members of your house to stay quiet and leave you alone.

Now, focus on a place inside yourself where you feel safe. When you have that place, describe it to yourself. Either the person with you can write it down or you can speak it out load into your recording device. Then, as you are in that safe place inside yourself, focus and concentrate on a memory in which you felt completely safe. When you can truly feel that feeling of feelings safe inside yourself, give that feeling a color and shape. Symbolize it. That makes the feeling tangible and physical. What is the color and shape of that feeling of safety? Repeat this process with feelings of security, protected, fulfilled, confidence, or whatever feelings you want to experience. I usually start with feeling safe, secure, and protected because I have noticed when a person has those feelings inside the mind can be more free and quiet. The feeling can be more centered and peaceful.

Now, let us suppose you would like to increase the attachment of mind stimulants or basic motives to your goals or chief aim in life. Here is an activity you could do with that goal in mind. First, let us choose the emotion of love to deeper connect our goal or aim. Next, remember a time in your life when you felt love. As you feel that feeling of love, take that feeling of love you feel inside yourself and give it both a color and a shape. Then, you could think of a time when you where listening to your favorite piece of music. Focus in on that feeling you have when you listen to your favorite piece of music, and give that feeling a color and shape (i.e., you give that feeling a symbol). You can repeat this process with any of the basic motives or mind stimulants you wish. You may even wish to add others of your choosing. I would encourage you to focus on positive emotions and experiences such as love and music rather than ones such as revenge or intoxication.

Having those symbols, imagine yourself holding them in your imaginary hands. Then imagine the end result of your goals or definite chief aim. Notice how you feel when you add your symbols to that completed end result of your goals or definite chief aim. Having this image of those symbols (which represent various feelings) placed within your end result of your goal or aim should help you feel more motivated and interested to keep your mind focused on your goal or aim.

There are other processes by which one could use this process, such as to eliminate fears. But space may limit the presentation.

Now, I would encourage or challenge you to ask yourself, "What do YOU think this secret is about which Hill wrote?" Whether or not you agree with me, I would encourage you explore two possibilities. The first possibility is that by asking yourself what this secret might be, you begin your own journey. I find answers come if I ask and expect guidance. By doing so, you may increase your self-reliance and may more easily find answers you seek in any area of your life. The second possibility I ask you upon which to take action is to do the activities listed within this chapter so that you may benefit from the information.

The edition used was the 1937 edition.

About Thomas Brown

As of November 10, 2010, Thomas Brown, Psy.D. has a doctorate degree in psychology and has a private practice in Orem, Utah. He is the overseer of Omni Research Foundation. He can be reached in the United States at (801) 404-2685 or at browntm@pacificu.edu. To call from another country, please check international calling instructions from your country to the United States.

> A thought thus "magnetized" with emotion may be compared to a seed which, when planted in fertile soil, germinates, grows, and multiplies itself over and over again, until that which was originally one small seed becomes countless millions of seeds of the same brand!
> —NAPOLEON HILL

12

A Touch of Genius

by Michael S. Johnson
AUSTRALIA

May 1980. Sydney, Australia. And 40 year old Lanky Bill was down on his luck. A recent business promotion of his *one-man-band* style business had failed leaving his bank accounts lean and dry. Short of cash.

His next promotion? His next job? Not even in his mind, yet. The last one had failed, and though it is possible that every failure has within itself the seed of an equivalent benefit . . . he couldn't see that either . . . yet.

Had lady fortune deserted him? For some days it appeared she had.

Until the day he "Just got lucky" as he said later, when he found a 2nd hand copy of *Think and Grow Rich* by Napoleon Hill for just $2 at a Sunday market.

Until destiny tapped him on the shoulder. Until he decided to reach for the stars . . .

Whoa . . . let's not jump forward. . . . Let's take this story one step at a time.

Lanky Bill did not emphatically believe one could *Think and Grow Rich.*

Loved the title, of course. Who wouldn't? But his negative inner voice said: *"Surely not . . . it can't be that easy."* How can one *Think and Grow Rich?* If we could all do this, there wouldn't be enough consumables on the planet for everyone.

With that *limiting thought,* he read it *lightly, quickly,* with a little skepticism.

He did agree with the philosopher in many ways: disagreed in others. And some sounded too mystical to be real. How could thoughts be things?

The hidden secret intrigued him. But he did not find it on his first reading.

He moved on with his life. Placed the book out of sight on his bookshelf, with the dismissive thought that: *"One can't get rich just by reading a book anyway."*

A week later Bill was, a little broker, cash-broker that is, and in need of a new money making goal.

He meditated.

Without warning intuition tapped him on the shoulder, and the *quiet voice within,* the one he sometimes listened to, the voice that was always intuitively correct, told him to read *Think and Grow Rich* again: which he did. This time with more patience as he mulled over what he was reading, a lot of which still sounded like fantasy to him.

Desire was stirring within.

What really fascinated him was the author's claim that the "secret" appeared over 100 times in the book. That the reader had to be *ready* to receive it before it became evident—and the claim that half of the secret was already in the reader's mind.

A thought passed his mind that "being ready" and knowing one was "ready" might be the secret. But no . . . it couldn't be that simple could it? He felt "ready" but nothing was happening in his life.

Bill was by nature quite a positive thinker. He was the man in charge of his own small business and lived by his wits. But he wasn't making a fortune. He wasn't an authentic entrepreneur, although he had desires in that direction. He had successes and he had failures.

Being a true shy-guy kind of person he ran a genuine one-man business: free-lance copywriting, and farming-out his secretarial and artwork requirements to nearby businesses. He also worked a few mail order business strategies of his own: selling "reports" and "newsletters" and "mini books" of his own creation. This was the business he loved and he also had "clients" for whom he acted as advertising agent, creating newspaper and magazine advertising. And he had a pleasing personality.

Sometimes he worked 60 or 70 hours a week and wondered if hard work alone was enough to make a fortune? Napoleon Hill said not. But hinted strongly that ideas were the starting point of all achievements.

Bill certainly worked hard but did not make big serious money. Until he understood *Think and Grow Rich*, he did not believe that one could, in truth, *Think and Grow Rich*. He believed more in the practical world of small business: exchanging service and product for the equivalent in cash . . . until the incredible day he had an implosion in his mind and received an idea that he acted on immediately. An idea that, without using *Think and Grow Rich* principles, would have remained as an unused idea—as most ideas do to so many people.

The secret intrigued him.

What was this secret that the author mentioned? What was the part that he already possessed? How could having a Definite Major Purpose change what he accepted as *now,* to what he wanted as the *now* of the future. He mused over the Definite Major Purpose theme for a long time and didn't really want to change the purpose he already had. He enjoyed his work. He simply wanted his purpose to yield more of the world's possessions to him. "Perhaps" he thought . . . "I am guilty of thinking small." Perhaps that was the secret.

The secret continued to intrigue Lanky Bill.

He read the author's preface again and again and again.

QUOTE:

In every chapter mention has been made of the money making secret which has made fortunes for more than 500 exceedingly wealthy men whom I have carefully analyzed over a long period of years. The secret was brought to my attention by Andrew Carnegie more than a quarter of a century ago. The secret to which I refer has been mentioned no fewer than 100 times throughout this book. It has not been directly named for it seems to work more successfully, when it is merely uncovered and left in sight, where THOSE WHO ARE READY and SEARCHING FOR IT may pick it up. That is why Mr. Carnegie tossed it to me so quietly, without giving me its specific name.

If you are READY to put it to use you will recognize the secret at least once in every chapter. I wish I might feel privileged to tell you how you will know if you are ready, but that would deprive you of much of the benefit you will receive when you make the discovery in your own way.

There is no such thing as something for nothing! The secret to which I refer cannot be had without a price, although the price is far less than its value. It cannot be had at any price by those who are not intentionally searching for it. It cannot be given away. It cannot be purchased for money, for the reason it comes in two parts. One part is already in possession of those who are ready for it.

UNQUOTE.

Oh how those few words intrigued Lanky Bill. These few sentences fascinated him so much that he read them again and again and again.

What was the secret?

How did it come in two parts?

How did one know when one was ready?

Why could it not be bought if 500 successful millionaires already knew and used it?

Why was it in the book 100 times when he could not even find it once?

Was it nothing more than a publisher's hoax to sell more books? Bill couldn't tell.

He took two days off from his work and read, absorbed and assimilated just a little of Napoleon Hill's principles. Looking to find the secret just once. And failing.

Or so he thought.

On the third day of absorbing *Think and Grow Rich*, the voice within said:

"Try it Bill. Maybe it really is true. Maybe you can *Think and Grow Rich*. Maybe the first step is having a Definite Major Purpose. If not, what have you got to lose by trying? If it's wrong you lose nothing. But what if it's right?"

Bill listened to the voice within and, in his work journal wrote his first Definite Major Purpose.

I WANT TO EARN A HALF A MILLION DOL-
LARS IN A SINGLE MONTH, THEN MOVE TO THE
GOLD COAST TO BEGIN A NEW LIFE.

And fell into hysterical laughter at the thought. At the idea
that he could do this in a month. In 1980 half a million dollars
was a whole lot of money.

Was the universe listening to him? Or was it laughing along
with him. Bill didn't know. But the book told him to *"begin
now whether he felt ready or not,"* so he began the "6 Steps" as
outlined by Napoleon Hill that very night.

In his youth Lanky Bill had been around the world several
times as a ship's radio officer, before deciding, at age 30, that
there must be a better life ashore. Odd jobs took him from
radio technician to salesman to futures market investor to
professional gambler where his natural mathematical skills
gave him an excellent edge.

Eventually he worked as creative author and advertising
person which suited him most.

In 1980 a TV quiz show, where one could win over a million dollars, was immensely popular in Australia. Object: to
win a million, and to do this the contestant had to be successful several nights in succession against very keen competition,
and the big prize only went off about twice a year.

Round about this time a charming European competitor,
Pierre, turned up in April, with a seductive French accent,
oodles of handsome smiles at which the ladies swooned, and
scooped the pool, taking out a cool million dollars. Millions
watched the final and Pierre was an instant celebrity. Pierre
was also an astute businessman.

Bill, at that time, was mailing out advertising to carefully
selected mailing lists, which seldom worked as well as he
expected, mainly because the lists of assembled names were

not guaranteed to be the type of people who would buy by mail, such lists being rare in Australia at that time. But he used these mail outs to improve his newly developing skills as a copywriter.

One day the list-broker that marketed these "lists" rang Bill to say that, after his big TV show win, businessman Pierre had capitalized on his new found fame and sold via newspapers and magazines a huge quantity of a book on "How I created my own Luck Cycle to Make a Million Dollars." His mail order publishers charged only $20 for this book and it was literally selling like crazy. Sales had gone through 100,000 in 6 weeks and the name list of those buyers was available from the agency.

Another of the list broker's clients had come up with the idea of getting Pierre to dictate a book and he—the promoter—had turned this booklet into $2,000,000—more than twice what Pierre had made on the TV show. Now the names were for sale. "Not a bad idea"—thought Bill when he heard about it. "Wish I'd thought of that."

Was this opportunity knocking on Lanky Bill's door?

Bill knew that the list was hot but he didn't have a suitable product. Nor did he have any money for a promotion. However he did know that people who bought a product like "Luck Cycle" were quite likely to buy another book of similar nature. The list broker's minimum order was 5000 names and the list was available to other marketers also. To take advantage of this new list, Bill knew he would have to get in early before the names had been hit by offer after offer after offer, which was likely to happen in the next few months. Normally Bill would have tried 5000 names . . . imagine his surprise when he heard himself ask the broker:

"Has it been sold yet?"

"No!"

"OK. How much would the entire list cost?"

"$20,000" came the reply.

"I'll take them," he answered, startled at his own temerity.

Without thinking of where the money would come from, or what he would sell, Bill was hit with the notion of marketing the whole list, the 100,000 people. His instant idea was to sell a product for $500, unheard of at that time. A product he did not have.

What he did have though was an idea.

Of course there were some massive problems looming. Lack of money. Lack of product. Lack of skills to do a promotion of this size. Lack of a story to tell. And no one had offered a book for $500 before. Oh! Oh! the doubts of disbelief almost overcame his intuitive "I'll take them" and negatives started to dance before his eyes.

Ignoring the negatives Bill recalled that Napoleon Hill had said: "When riches begin to come, they come so quickly, in such great abundance, that one wonders where they have been hiding during all those lean years."

Didn't sound like the secret. More like "after the secret."

He found that quote inspiring and settled back to do the mathematics, pausing at times to visualize riches arriving in abundance.

To buy the list $20,000. Printing costs say $75,000. Postage $45,000. They are the big 3. Inserting/folding delivery costs unknown (check it out). . . . Product and fulfillment costs unknown (check it out). . . . Artwork . . . unknown. Writing high quality sales letter ($6000 quoted). Make that FREE— he thought—what the heck he would do that himself.

"Maybe $180,000 will cover it all" he calculated.

Now Lanky Bill did not have a product. Lanky Bill did not have any money in the bank . . . two items that would have turned back many a lesser man. But Lanky Bill surprised himself the next morning when he rang the list-broker back and authorized

$20,000 from his credit card to buy the 100,000 name list. He had taken the first step . . . ready or not. He had commitment. Now he had a $20,000 debt against an asset of 100,000 hot buyers' names. Without realizing it, his Definite Major Purpose was coming to life.

Perhaps taking the first step was action. Was that the secret? Without knowing why he felt inspired.

His first call was to a business that inserted/folded/arranged bulk mailings, etc. They would do the job but wanted their $50,000 which included postage, before delivering to the mail centre. No deposit. No job.

Suddenly Bill came back down to earth with the realization that maybe he was being a dreamer. He had a good idea, he'd invested $20,000 borrowed dollars on his credit cards, but he didn't have any money for follow up or even a product. And what if the printer wouldn't give him credit? The negatives started piling up in his imagination.

All he really had was an idea, a debt and a Definite Major Purpose.

Contemptuously he threw the negatives aside, remembering the story of the general who arrived on foreign shores with a handful of soldiers. The general sent his men ashore to fight an enemy that outnumbered them 5 to 1. The general, a great man of action, promptly set his boats on fire, and told his astonished and outnumbered troops. . . . "This is the point of no return. . . . We win or we perish. . . ."

History records that they won.

"What the heck" ruminated Bill. "My boats are burned. Let's go all the way and do this promotion."

He took his next step up the ladder.

What a great decision. Well done Lanky Bill. You reached the point of no return and kept on marching.

Into the valley of death . . . rode the 600.

Next stop, Bill discussed printing an *estimated* 10 page sales letter and envelope with his printer and came up with a cost, payable at the end of the month. That gave him breathing space. He was still about $50,000 short of go ahead money to get things under way. Credit was fine but he needed a cash guarantee for immediate confirmation of everything. He could not continue without that extra $50,000.

He phoned his friendly bank manager, making an appointment for later that day. His interview went something like this:

"Ronald I need $50,000 for promotional purposes."

"OK Bill, how long do you want it for?"

"A month will be fine . . ."

"Consider it done. The money will be in your account tomorrow morning, standard overdraft interest rates will apply."

"Thanks Ronald."

Bill was out on the street in less than 4 minutes with $50,000 in the bank.

Next day there was $50,000 in the bank.

He had taken his next step up the ladder of success. Using OPM. Other people's money.

Impossible? Not in 1980. Banks had money to burn at that time.

Frightening stuff, but this was Bill's first entrepreneurial strategy, and he knew there was more to it than "just money"— real, borrowed or paper.

Weeks later when the whole project was completed Bill took his bank manager out for lunch and he asked him: *"Ronald, why did you lend me that $50,000 without any queries?"*

The manager smiled back and said: *"It was the look in your eyes.* I saw that you were determined to get the money somewhere, somehow, so I lent it to you. I sensed that you were focused on something big and I sensed that money was only a part of it. I trusted you to honor your commitment."

Bill did not have a sales letter. Nor did he have a product. He decided to give the product a name for now, and write the letter first.

He called his product "A Touch of Genius."

Wise decision. He had taken his next step up the ladder of success.

Of course the real Touch of Genius came from Bill himself. For the first time in a long time he had a Definite Major Purpose. He wanted to make half a million dollars in a month and move to a new state to live—and to do this he had to find or create a product for which he could ask $500—and he had to write a letter brilliant enough to sell enough product to pay all his rapidly expanding costs and give him a profit. His mathematics told him he needed to make about 400 sales of A Touch of Genius to break even. As his figures showed that was only .4 of 1% of the 100,000.

Lanky Bill had the passion to do it.

He had taken his next step up the ladder of success.

He was literally ablaze with enthusiasm. Inside him a fire was burning that nothing would diminish. He never stopped for a moment to think of the negatives. He never considered the tiniest possibility of failure. He didn't think that *maybe no one will buy a book for $500 from a complete stranger who wrote them a letter.*

He started writing and never stopped for four full days. He wrote. He edited. He corrected. He checked. He improved. And wrote again. His objective was to create such a burning desire in his readers hearts that they would happily send him their $500. They had to want A Touch of Genius more than they wanted their money to remain in their wallets. Bill's letter had to move his dream from him to his reader without sounding like incredible hype or Get Rich Quick.

Bill wanted his readers to understand the benefits available from owning A Touch of Genius. That's what he sold: benefits . . . benefits . . . benefits and more benefits. Each new benefit gave him a new point to make in his yet to be written book. This is so astonishing that, later the next week, he simply took his advertising letter and wrote the benefits into the product, easily, effortlessly, almost automatically. The book wrote itself to fit the advertising letter.

By the time he finished his sales letter it was 15 pages long when he sent it out to the local layout shop and secretarial service for the final type. He considered shortening it to save printing costs but his inner voice said: *"Don't do that Bill . . . it's fine the way it is."*

Would people read a letter that long? His inner voice said they would. Maybe listening to the inner voice is the secret? But he hadn't read that in the book.

What he had done though was taken his next step up the ladder of success.

Before the final copy was prepared Bill showed it to two close friends. He asked them to read the sales letter and tell him if it was clear. Not did they like it or not like it. Simply did they understand exactly what was on offer and how to obtain it? They were both sure the letter was clear. The copy was good. One said he would buy it and one said he would not. The one who wanted to buy it looked staggered when Bill said: "Oh I haven't written it yet. . . . This is a back to front project. First I have a market of people who may buy it. . . . Now I have the letter to send to them . . . and finally I shall fulfill my end of the deal by creating and sending buyers the product."

"But shouldn't one have a product first and then look for a buyer?"

"Perhaps . . ." Bill thought . . . "Perhaps . . ." Not allowing anything to distract him from his focused attention to detail as he marched on with fulfillment of his Definite Major Purpose.

A peek at Bill's copy now.

Lanky Bill wrote of how A Touch of Genius could teach readers how to generate $60,000 from a single idea. And if that idea was too big for them to grasp . . . How to make $5000 in a single weekend. Lanky Bill described A Touch of Genius as being New, Unique, Scientifically Proven but Practical, Sensible, Down-to-Earth. A thinking man's tool for creating multiple streams of income, whatever one's background may have been.

Bill promised to reveal all the ways he knew to get a personal edge in gambling markets. He would take his readers step by step through the system he had used to make profits 75% of the time at the races in his days as a professional gambler. And reveal new secrets of a unique way of playing the stock futures markets, where one only traded 4 times a year and the averages showed 3 out of the 4 times to be successful. And he talked glowingly of the law of expansion that would enable readers to move from one product to another, accumulating as they speculated so that riches in scientific gambling could indeed be theirs.

As Bill passionately told his readers

Today truly is the first day of the rest of your life.

Today is your lucky day.

Today is the day good fortune smiles upon you.

Today must be your day of action.

Today is your magic "Do it now day."

Today is the day when you begin to take steps to turn your ideas, your plans, your birthright of success, your creativity, into your future . . . using the magic formulas I have outlined in *A Touch of Genius.*

Today is the day you empower yourself by getting your hands on this new exciting life changing book. A manual that will completely shatter all the mysterious old myths of success and reveal how you—especially you— can become a perpetual, total and continuous winner!

Additionally to these urges to action he had to excite his readers, so he told them the story of how he received his greatest idea.

I TAKE A BATH!

A few years ago, during one of the most desperate financial periods of my life, I spent one entire day trying to find ways to make money.

I just "sat" and "thought" for ideas. Maybe you'd call it meditation.

After hours of this, I gave up, and exhausted, decided to take a bath. That was the greatest bath I ever took in my life! As I lay there trying to relax away my problems and worries, I suddenly received a revelation. I can call it nothing else but a "miracle," a gift from the storehouse of all knowledge, the universe, linked in unknown ways to my subconscious mind. For that "miracle" that "aha" was the basis of A Touch of Genius—the greatest breakthrough in creative money making this century for me! It was my stock market trading idea and this too will be revealed to you in

"A TOUCH OF GENIUS"

Bill also told a few stories to show how the great can make mistakes, while the man in the street—in this instance a barber—can be smart and successful.

Do bad past experiences influence your future directions? Many people feel emotional about their past experiences and are unable to let them go, allowing past bad experiences to influence the present and the future.

Let them go

Mark Twain, a famous American 19th Century writer, yet a simple man of the people, was sitting on his veranda one evening having a beer with his neighbor, who happened to be his local barber. A smartly dressed salesman called and was invited to sit and join them and make his presentation.

The salesman went to great lengths to explain that he represented a business company, marketing shares in a new product. A new invention that was going to take the world by storm, and would make thousands of people wealthy, and possibly millions of dollars for those who helped to finance the new business now, by buying shares.

An angry Mark Twain chased the man off his veranda.

"Get out of here. I've been caught before with these crazy wild share schemes. Why just last year I bought a whole heap of x shares in a new company and within a very few months the company had folded up and I lost all my money.

"I will never buy shares again."

The embarrassed salesman left and the barber neighbor escorted him off the premises. However the barber, who had not had a bad shares experience, was very interested in what he had heard, and invited the salesman to his place, next door, where he listened to the story again.

The barber bought into the company and made millions.

Mark Twain made nothing!

Although the company was selling a brilliant new invention, a bad experience in Mark's past influenced his reception to the salesman's new ideas.

The famous Mark Twain allowed the emotions of a bad past experience to reach into the present and influence a decision that could effect his future.

Time proved him wrong.

Don't do this! Don't let your personal past influence your emotions or decisions today. Evaluate on the present and learn how to influence your own future, now, today!

You know if the bad experiences of yesterday truly influenced people to act on them, no one would get married twice. Life's not like that! We are human, we are romantics, we are emotional dreamers, we are ambitious, we are optimists, we think that "*This time it will be better*" and people get married again and again and again and again, always believing that the new experience will be better than a bad one that took place in the past.

And so it should be.

The invention Mark Twain refused and which his barber bought into was Bell Telephone one of the greatest inventions of all time.

Lanky Bill began another series of urges to action. Followed by more stories.

Like the imaginary man who wrote Bill a letter of thanks:

QUOTE

Bill—

For years now I dreamed a dream of getting out of the area I live in. An area full of unemployed people and thieves. Don't ask how I got here. That's another long story.

You know Bill I have to lock up my garden hose or someone will steal it, even while I am still at home. My kids had their bikes pinched, I lost an old car, and I was burgled 3 times in the last year and I am screaming in my mind to find a way to get out of this problem area. To live in a better neighborhood.

All I wanted was what you described as a "passport to success" and I thank you from the bottom of my heart that I obtained your incredible Touch of Genius. I needed it desperately. I couldn't afford it. But I read your letter and I made myself afford it. And I thank the Lord for this gift that is changing my life each and every day I live . . . Thank you Bill. You're a wonderful man.

UNQUOTE

Now there is a little creative "author's license" there, a touch more freedom to write creatively than is available today. But the desperate man was really Bill. His boats were burning. He had passed the point of no return. He had to succeed or die.

Bill continued his amazing letter:

You know *I truly want to share A Touch of Genius with you.*

It's your master plan not mine.

I am only a humble collector of valuable information. And I want you to have this valuable information too—To discover your way to be wealthy.

For you can do this too.

You owe yourself and your family the chance to change your life for the better.

You owe it to yourself to have a new stream of income.

Imagine where you can go in the future if you have successful money making plans in place on a continual basis.

Imagine a plan that will make you money in Spring, Summer, Autumn or Winter?

The genius is truly yours. Only you can do it! No one else. Only you.

Yes, Bill poured his burning passion into this sales letter asking readers:

Ever wondered about people who get rich overnight?

The people who are blessed with more talent and personality than you?

Those who don't deserve it but get the promotions anyway?

The people who are happier and luckier than others?

Or are born into the luxury of unearned wealth? Well I'm telling it like it is right now when I say that you can join them regardless of your age, sex, personality or education, past failures or present position.

YOU NEED A PLAN. Starting today. And A Touch of Genius is that plan.

It is actually simpler than you can ever imagine. You can have everything you ever wanted quickly, easily, effortlessly, once you have a plan. And work that plan.

Lanky Bill then dampened the fire a little:

Look I'm not promising you a ticket to easy street. You still have to do a little work and make simple intelligent decisions.

I'm not suggesting that this is everything you need to know to be a raging success in life.

I'm not telling you that this is the secret weapon of tycoons. Nor is it a license to print money. And it may not make you the richest person on your street.

What I am saying, and I hope I am saying it clearly, is that the plan works! It will work for you, and will make you some serious money, if you are prepared to work it sensibly.

So don't waste one more minute. Read on and I will soon show you how to get your copy of the limited edition version of A Touch of Genius.

In finishing Bill reminded his readers that:
Life's battles don't always go
To the stronger or faster man
But sooner or late the man who wins
Is the man who thinks he can.

Bill was staggered when, a week later, he paid his $50,000 to the forwarding house and staggered to see the size of the two trucks of palletted mail ready to be moved to the postal authorities. Staggered to think that all this came from a simple idea. An idea that was yet to be proven.

He had more costs of course. His letter ended up 50% bigger than his original plans but he wouldn't shorten it. His intuition, his inner voice said no. It felt right. The simple ungrammatical me-to-you letter was Bill's way of reaching people. Didn't sound too fancy. Higher printing costs OK. The forwarding house told him there were 3000 names for New Zealand in the 100,000 and that would cost him an extra $3000. The inner voice said that was OK too. And a little "trick" he had learned at a seminar of adding a bright blue insert to his mail out cost him more again. He also decided to add an additional order form in a different colour—as well as the one printed on the last page. This made it easier for people to buy. Again he listened to his intuition. A return envelope was added and his artwork friend created a new business letterhead especially for this product. And did a clever letter layout before it was typed. More cost. More potential. More making it easy to order.

He listened to his subconscious. Maybe that was the secret?

His debts were over $180,000 or $1.80 for each envelope mailed out. Return to break even 360 x $500 plus a bit more for interest and product and fulfillment costs. His original mathematics had said .4 of 1% and he was within his estimates. His organized planning was proving to be correct.

Lastly Bill estimated the date he would mail out and added a PS that the offer would expire 14 days after that date. That went on the bright blue insert. Every reader was guaranteed to know of the offer expiry date. He was putting them in the position of a point of no return and burning boats.

This was his final urge to action . . . he was truly committed. Eventually the copy was finished. It was as said a simple
me-to-you letter from one friend to another. Bill took it to his
printer.

A Touch of Genius—the book

Bill now poured every emotion he had into producing a fine
quality A4 Manual. He wrote for 12 hours a day every day
for 6 days. As weariness overcame him, but suddenly it was
finished. Every money making technique and tactic he had
ever tried he put down on paper. There were no computers
for reference in those days. All he had was his own life time
experiences.

Lanky Bill had his manual professionally typed and
ordered 1000 copies. Another $10,000. Had an imitation
leather cover made. Another $6000.

Three days after the mailing there were 4 replies. Next day
40, then a flood over the next two weeks. In total 1,247 orders.
No one was happier than Lanky Bill when he paid the printer
and ordered a second printing of his book. And paid his bank.
And the small business people like the artwork guy and the
typist.

Of the 1,247 buyers 4 people asked for a refund which had
not been promised or mentioned. They promptly received it.
Lanky Bill believed in The Golden Rule.

He had taken his next step up the ladder of success.

Bill's debts were all paid on time and yet the half a million
dollars was not quite achieved.

His phone rang.

"There are another 40,000 names available if you want
them?" said the list broker.

"I'll take them" replied Bill, and although they didn't respond quite as well as the original 100,000, his extra sales ensured that he did make his half a million in just over a month.

When this first big promotion was over, Bill drove up to the Gold Coast in his new red Porsche sports car with his trusted typewriter on the back seat.

On the 1000 mile drive he had time to think about his new mail order entrepreneur's lifestyle.

Time to think.

Had he discovered the secret? He went over *Think and Grow Rich* in his mind.

Bill had a **Definite Major Purpose** which he wrote down in line with **Napoleon Hill's 6 Steps that Turn Desire into Gold**. The instructions for the 6 steps stated were to **began right away**, whether he was ready or not. He had. Was this the secret?

Perhaps **being ready** was writing down one's **Definite Major Purpose** and using the **6 steps** in accordance with the instructions in *Think and Grow Rich*. Was this the secret? Perhaps this was half of it?

Had he used a **Master Mind Alliance**? No he didn't think he had, but he had used **Teamwork** and worked in **a spirit of friendly cooperation** with a List Broker, a Bank Manager, a Printer, an Artwork Person, a Typist, a Mailing House, all of whom had performed their skilled tasks to his instructions.

Perhaps teamwork was the secret?

Had he **applied faith**? Yes he had faith in his **right idea at the right time** from the moment when he said *"I'll take them"* to his list broker. His **faith** had removed the "can't be done" thinking that had entered his mind on the first day. And the project had kept him so busy he didn't have time for the negatives.

Perhaps that was the secret . . . being creatively busy?

Did he work with a pleasing personality? Perhaps? In reality he had been too focused. Too determined to succeed. His personality had taken a back seat for the journey. Or had it come through in his words?

Did he use **personal initiative**? Yes he did. He recognized an opportunity that millions might have missed. And from that day on he has found that he has been **surrounded by opportunities every day of his life**, opportunities that he previously may not have recognized.

Was the secret that simple? **Recognizing opportunities?**

Was the secret **enthusiasm**? Lanky Bill qualified on this one. In fact passionate may be more the word. He had worked passionately and enthusiastically ignoring all negatives until the job was done.

Did he exercise **self discipline**? Yes he did. He kept his mind on the job. On what he wanted and off the negatives of what he did not want. This was also **accurate thinking**. And **controlled attention**.

Remember Rocky said: *"It isn't the number of times that you get knocked down that makes you a winner . . . it's the number of times you get up and start again."*

Did Bill use **creative vision**? Yes he did. From the moment he said **I have a Definite Major Purpose** to the time he said *"I'll take them"* he worked with creative vision, **listening to his intuitive voice within** also.

Did it all begin with an idea? Yes it did. Was the idea invisible? Yes. Was the idea a thought? Yes. Did the thought become a thing? Yes. Was the action that turned that thought into a thing the secret?

Going through all this stuff in his mind, Bill kept on asking himself, "**What is the secret that is mentioned over 100 times** in the book *Think and Grow Rich?*" He thought, "I must have absorbed it somehow as I turned an empty bank account into half a million in just over a month. But I still don't know what the secret is."

Then he remembered a story he had heard of Henry Ford telling someone who was marveling about his millions and asking what he would do if he lost everything.

Henry's reply was *"I'd have it all back in 4 or 5 years"*

Ford obviously knew the secret.

Bill wasn't sure if that story was true . . . or possible . . . but he suspected it was . . . until he realized that somewhere in the last few months, somewhere in his recent success, his thinking had changed. He had a residual **success consciousness** now, an **imprinted belief**. He no longer missed opportunities. He no longer thought that any idea was too big for him. He was an entrepreneur who could take an idea and turn it into a success story. He knew he would succeed again and again and again. And in bigger more exciting ways than ever before.

Was that the secret?

A knowing, a faith, that one could succeed whatever the circumstances that surrounded one. As long as one maintained a **success consciousness** at all times, there was no horizon too distant, no goal too big to be achieved.

Faith alone may not be sufficient. To succeed again and again one needs to use, whenever possible, all the 13 principles of Napoleon Hill and deliver them in one's life in the spirit of the Golden Rule.

Bill arrived at the Gold Coast and told a friend of his experiences.

Bill went on and on making a long story of it.

His friend became exasperated. "Well Bill, come on . . . what is the secret . . . ?"

"I don't know" answered Bill. "But I can give you a book where it is mentioned 100 times."

"Meanwhile . . . I'll be busy working on my new Definite Major Purpose. This time I'm going for a million."

About Michael S. Johnson

Michael S. Johnson is an Australian author/editor/ publisher of direct response advertising and newsletters. Now retired to a tropical beach he continues to write and trade and practices the "give before you get" principles in his everyday life. He can be reached on www.michaels johnson.com.

13

What is the "secret" in Think and Grow Rich that Napoleon Hill refers to and is supposedly said on every page of the book?

by Raymond Campbell
LAKE ORION, MICHIGAN

After studying and speaking to hundreds of the world's most successful people, Napoleon Hill wrote *Think and Grow Rich*. In this classic book, Hill shares the secrets to success—the things that Henry Ford, Thomas Edison and so many others did to become successful. But the most compelling secret appears in the title. The most useful secret, the secret used by all the hundreds of persons studied by Hill, is the first word in the title of his book—THINK!

I suspect that most people focus on the last 2 words in the title, **Grow Rich**, giving too little attention to that all important first word—THINK. I believe that using the word THINK is Hill's way of focusing the reader's attention on all the mental processes that are required to become successful. Hill makes this clear as the book unfolds.

Hill repeatedly writes about the importance of a definite major purpose in our lives, a burning desire, a positive mental attitude, and that whatever the mind can conceive and believe the mind can achieve. Beliefs, desires, attitudes, ideas, recognizing opportunities, motivation, and so on all have their origins in one's mind. These are mental activities that move us towards success. Each one of these essential activities begins in the MIND. Being so, it is altogether accurate for Hill to entitle his book *THINK and Grow Rich*.

Since what one focuses on, thinks and believes may propel that person to success, it is also true that the improper use of one's mind may lead to mediocrity or even worse. My experience parallels Hill's instructions: What we think about, what we focus on, what we tell ourselves and what we believe, will all work together to influence what we achieve in life. If we exercise positive control over what we "feed" our minds, what we allow our minds to focus on and believe, then we can achieve great things.

Correspondingly, if we do not control our minds, if we do not discipline our minds to focus on our most important goals, if we do not use our minds to energize our efforts, if we waste our mental energies on the inane and irrelevant or on coarse gossip and the denigration of others, then we are wasting and misusing our mental powers. It should be no surprise that one who invests his/her energy into such meaningless activities is not likely to experience great success. So, to those ambitious few in every generation, who want much more out of life, I provide the following exercise. I can introduce you to Napoleon Hill's timeless and proven techniques by encouraging you to THINK about your answers to the following questions:

+ What do you want to be?
+ What do you want to do with your life?
+ What do you want to achieve in life?
+ What do you want to be known for?
+ What are you very good at doing?
+ What do you do that gives you the most pleasure?
+ Do you have a smoldering, persistent desire to do something that is different than what you do today? What is that secret desire?
+ Imagine that it is many years from now and you are nearing your final years. As you review your entire life, what memories or achievements would make you think, "Yes, I was very successful! It has been a full and gratifying life."
+ In brief: What do you want? When do you want it?

If these questions can help you to determine your Definite Major Purpose in life, then you have THOUGHT it through and now have a compelling reason to apply Hill's other principles—so that you can achieve your Major Purpose in life.

Do not be surprised if you find that Hill's other secrets and suggestions require THINKING, too (i.e., using your MIND in powerful, goal-oriented, constructive, positive and action-oriented ways).

Perhaps you are one of those rare individuals who want more out of life. Like Napoleon Hill, and so many other successful people, you realize that your *mind* (i.e., your thoughts, ideas, desires, values, motivation, goals, etc.) is your strongest and best ally on the Battlefield of Life.

If you want to achieve more in life, if you want more out of life, if you want to realize your Major Purpose in life, then you need to become the **master** of your *mind.*

If you want to know how to become master of your mind, you need to know how to manage and channel your mind's power. You need to know how to get your mind working for you, not against you. If the preceding describes you, read on!

We <u>Become</u> What We THINK About: 5 Powerful Lessons

I know that the 5 Lessons I share below are important and that they will work for you! How do I know? Because these 5 Lessons have worked for me!

By most measures, I have had a very successful life. After serving as a combat soldier in Vietnam, I returned home to lead a positive, productive life that included many personal and professional accomplishments.

I came back from Vietnam with a plan. My plan included the following:

+ Study Accounting.
+ Become a Certified Public Accountant.
+ Own and operate my own successful business.
+ Get married to my high school sweetheart.
+ Become a father to happy children who become assets to society.
+ Build my own building.
+ Work out of that building with my children.
+ Help other businesses and business persons to succeed.
+ Make a positive impact on my community and my country.

I have achieved every item on that plan and, in some cases, I have far exceeded those goals. Why? Because I learned to *master my mind* by applying these 5 Lessons:

Lesson 1: Thoughts are POWERFUL Things.
Lesson 2: Inside each of us are 2 people.
Lesson 3: You CONTROL your thoughts.
Lesson 4: You have a CHOICE about what thoughts enter
and dominate your mind.
Lesson 5: You BECOME what you think about.

Lesson 1:
Thoughts are POWERFUL Things.

Thoughts are very powerful things! Thoughts are not just invisible, electrical impulses in your brain. Thoughts contain your insight, wisdom, experience, wants and desires.

Thoughts influence what you Believe and, therefore, thoughts influence what you will Achieve. So, thoughts help determine if you will succeed or not. If you BELIEVE that you can, and believe that you will succeed, you probably will!

Henry Ford, the great manufacturing giant said, "Whether you think you can or you think you can't, you're right!" Mr. Ford meant that if you THINK you CAN do something, you CAN and you will probably succeed. If you THINK you CAN NOT do something, you are right, you probably will NOT succeed.

Lesson 2: Inside each of us are 2 people:
A Positive Person and A Negative Person.

I've seen this in my own life. At times, I'm a positive person. In some cases, I've been a negative person. I can tell you from personal experience that the POSITIVE RAY was the most productive, the most successful and the most happy. The NEGATIVE RAY was less productive, less successful and less happy.

I believe that each person has the same challenge, the same duality: You are a Positive Person and you are a Negative

Person. The question IS: Which person is dominating your mind—the Positive You or the Negative You?

The answer to this question leads us to Lesson #3.

Lesson 3: You CONTROL your thoughts!

You can control if your thoughts are primarily Positive or Negative. Negativity is a habit—a very bad habit! Being positive is the very best habit of all!

Never let negative thoughts control you or your destiny. When you sense that negative ideas and thoughts are entering your mind, things that say "I Can't" or "I Won't Succeed," substitute them with positive thoughts as quickly as possible. Whatever you think about, you become. YOU can control your thoughts and what your mind dwells upon.

Lesson 4: You have a CHOICE about what thoughts enter and dominate your mind.

You are in control of your own mind. If you are in control, you have a choice. If you want to succeed, and think you can, you probably will. Only allow POSITIVE thoughts to control your mind. YOU are the Master of YOUR Mind.

Take CONTROL of your thoughts and CHOOSE to focus on positive thoughts and positive outcomes!

Lesson 5: You BECOME what you think about.

Whatever you allow your mind to focus on the most, that is what is most likely to come true.

What do successful people and star performers focus their minds upon? They constantly strive to remain positive. They write out specific goals and work to achieve their goals. They believe they can achieve their goals.

It is important to note that goals are important to very successful persons because they give a person purpose, focus and direction. Goals help them measure achievement and progress as they work towards realizing their Major Purpose. And achieving one's Major Purpose in life is what a positive, driven, success-oriented person focuses on and is thinking about all the time.

What do less successful people focus on? They tend to think in negative terms. They often think that they will not succeed or that there is "no use in even trying." They may think that there is no need to set goals. (I read once that less than 3% of the people in America establish measurable, written goals. Perhaps that is why only about 3% of the populace become very successful—they are the ones with written goals!)

Given a choice, and you and I always have a Choice (see Lesson 4), I'd much rather be the positive person who thinks I CAN and who works to achieve goals important to me! **How About You?**

Always remember:

If Positive thoughts dominate your mind—you win, you achieve, you succeed!

If Negative thoughts dominate your mind—you lose, you fail!

Want proof that these 5 Lessons work in the real world for real people? Read on!

The Phone Booth Story

Here's a true story that illustrates how these 5 Lessons were important in my life . . . and how they might change your life, too!

In 1967, I was 20 years old; I was standing in line, in a light rain, waiting to get into a phone booth to call my mother.

I had been inducted into the United States Army and had completed my basic training. I had just learned that I was being sent to Ft. Polk, Louisiana to learn how to become a combat soldier. After the Ft. Polk advanced infantry training, I would be sent to Vietnam. That's when I first met the Negative Me—the Negative Ray.

I was DEVASTATED! I was overwhelmed with negative thoughts and feelings. I asked myself: "Why Me? What did I do to deserve this? How was I going to tell my mother the worst message any mother could hear at that time—that her child was going to Vietnam to be a combat soldier?"

As I dialed mom's number, the negativity inside me continued to build. However, when I heard mom's voice, a change came over me . . . a great calmness came over me: I told mom that I was going to Ft. Polk, LA.

Mom asked, "Ray, what does that mean?" I told her that this meant that, "I would get the Best Training, from the Best Army, from the Best Country in the world and that, when I returned home from Vietnam as a combat soldier, I would go to college on the GI Bill."

When I was in Vietnam, I approached my job there with a Positive Focus. I didn't think exclusively about all the Negative influences around me.

I thought about going to college. I thought in detail about the courses I would take in Business, Mathematics and Accounting. I thought about the OUTCOMES I wanted like earning my CPA certification and opening my own business. I thought about marrying my high school sweetheart.

By the time I returned home from Vietnam, I had specific goals and a detailed plan in mind. I *did* go to college on the GI Bill. I *did* take courses in Accounting.

I *did* earn my CPA designation. I *did* open my own CPA business and I sold it later for a lot of money. And I *did* marry my high school sweetheart and we've been happily married for over 41 years!

I conceived my plan, I believed in it, I worked for it and it came true!

At the time, I didn't understand all the Positive and Negative phases I went through that rainy day in 1967 as I waited to call my mother. Several years later, when I read Napoleon Hill's book *Think and Grow Rich*, the pieces began to fit into place. And that book has helped me to be more successful ever since.

Think and Grow Rich was written in 1937 and it is as relevant and powerful today as it was when it was written over 70 years ago.

One of the main lessons in that book was that We Become What We Think About. That principle has been proven and re-proven to me over the past 40 years.

So, how did these 5 Lessons apply to my life and play themselves out over the next 40 years?

Lesson 1: Thoughts are POWERFUL Things.

As I stood in line waiting to call my mother in 1967, waiting to tell her news that she did not want to hear, I was overwhelmed with negative thoughts and feelings.

The Negativity was controlling my thoughts . . . and one negative thought led to another negative thought . . . it was like a horrible downward cycle that I did not think I could stop . . . the negativity fed on itself and became overwhelming . . . those negative thoughts were very powerful things!

Lesson 2: Inside each of us are 2 people: A Positive Person and a Negative Person.

Those negative thoughts and feelings brought out the Negative Ray. Everything was negative, I was in a cyclone of negativity. Negative experiences and outcomes were all I could think about. There was no room for the Positive Ray.

Lesson 3: YOU control your thoughts!

At the moment I heard my mother's voice I learned that I had CONTROL over my thoughts. I went from anxious to calm. I could focus on the positive or I could focus on the negative . . . I had Control. If I have Control, I have a Choice!

Lesson 4: You have a CHOICE about what thoughts enter and dominate your mind.

When speaking to my mother, I had the CHOICE of reporting all the negative thoughts and feelings I was experiencing, or I could switch gears and focus on the POSITIVE—the POSITIVE ideas of getting great training and, later, going to school and living out my dreams.

Lesson 5: You become what you think about.

While in Vietnam, my thoughts about going to school, opening my own business and getting married were so clear, so powerful, that I was compelled to execute them.

When I got home, I started to BECOME what I had thought about for all those months. I found that those positive thoughts were just as powerful as the negative thoughts, but the positive thoughts and dreams had much better outcomes and results.

Learning to focus on the Positive, and to apply the 5 Lessons we've described in this chapter, has served me well for decades.

And based on my experience, and the work of Napoleon Hill in *Think and Grow Rich*, I know that these 5 Lessons will serve you, your family and your co-workers well, too.

Here are a few questions for you to THINK about:

Q: Can you imagine being on the battlefield of Vietnam, Iraq or Afghanistan with a negative mental attitude? How could you focus on the life or death tasks that needed to be done?

I can tell you from personal experience, being Negative is NOT a good condition on the battlefield! A negative attitude causes . . .

+ Self-Doubt
+ Clouded Judgment
+ Fear
+ And, in many people, the Inability to Execute. A negative attitude causes a form of Paralysis when action is needed—the person is paralyzed and can NOT act.

Are negative thoughts any more helpful on the "Business Battlefield" or the "Battlefield of everyday Life?" No! You need a Positive Attitude in Business and in Life, too!

And when the STAKES are HIGH, that is when you especially need a Positive Attitude. In combat, on the battlefield, the stakes are very high, literally life or death—your very survival!

On the Business Battlefield, the stakes are high, too. The survival of your business. Your livelihood. The livelihood of your employees. Every employee's rent or mortgage payment. The ability to pay for food or the kids' education. These are high stakes indeed!

Q: Wouldn't it be great if your family or those in your work-place focused on Positive Thoughts and Positive Outcomes?

Imagine the difference it would make in your home life and work life if people around you focused on the Positive, not the negative!

Positive Thinking and a Positive Attitude are import-ant, but more is required to be successful. Being Successful requires Action—Positive Action! Discipline. Dedication. Practice. It requires replacing the old, ineffective habits of thinking negatively with new, effective habits of thinking pos-itively. It requires training yourself to think, to plan and to act in new, more constructive ways. It takes APPLICATION of these concepts to start to change your life for the better.

If you can start training your mind to focus on positive goals and positive outcomes, that is a great start. And the 5 Lessons I shared above will help you begin that process and take you to new levels of success!

Q: Do you want to change the direction, tone and outcomes of your life?

Q: Do you want to get more out of your business, your work-ers and your life?

Q: Do you want to enhance your relationships with family and friends?

Q: Do you want to realize YOUR Major Purpose in life?

It begins with a Positive Mental Attitude AND these 5 Les-sons. Then, you must be willing, dedicated, and have the desire to take your life to a new level. You MUST be focused.

You MUST be disciplined. You MUST work hard because success always requires hard work! Most importantly: You MUST *master your mind.*

This is so important that I named my business Mastermind Solutions. At Mastermind Solutions, for many decades, I have helped business professionals and entire companies to put these positive principles into practice. It is very gratifying to watch your client transform their business, their productivity, their profits and their lives! It is very rewarding to help others to *master their minds* and to *THINK and Grow Rich!*

Based on firsthand experience, and decades of research on the most successful people in the world, I can confidently tell you that Hill's book *Think and Grow Rich* and the 5 Lessons I shared in this chapter will help you to . . .

1. establish and realize YOUR goals and dreams
2. bring greater prosperity to YOU and YOUR family
3. bring greater happiness and fulfillment to YOU as a person.

Whatever the mind can conceive and believe the mind can achieve.

Positive thoughts, a positive outlook, coupled with positive action, will positively influence what you achieve in life. Why? Because thoughts are THINGS! Thoughts are VERY POWERFUL THINGS!

So powerful that Napoleon Hill put the Supreme Secret on every page of his book:

THINK AND GROW RICH!

About Raymond Campbell

Raymond Campbell is the President of Mastermind Solutions Inc., a management consulting firm in Lake Orion, Michigan specializing in creating and implementing management goals, metrics and tools that get results! Mr. Campbell is a Vietnam veteran, Certified Public Accountant, and a certified instructor for the Napoleon Hill World Learning Center. Ray is an ardent believer and teacher of the mastermind principle. You can reach him at www.mastermindsolutions.com.

Faith is the head chemist of the mind. When faith is blended with thought, the subconscious mind instantly picks up the vibration, translates it into its spiritual equivalent, and transmits it to Infinite Intelligence, as in the case of prayer.

–NAPOLEON HILL

14

When Defeat Barges In...

by Janet Jones
YORKSHIRE, ENGLAND

No one said that life was going to be easy. Everyone reaches a challenging time at some point in his or her life. 'This is an opportunity to grow,' they say. Within the works of Napoleon Hill lies the secret to 'growth.' The clue is in the title '*THINK and GROW Rich*.' This isn't a book just about strategies to make you financially rich. In the text, Napoleon Hill discusses the importance of giving back and being kind and considerate to others that are as much a part of being rich as having financial goals. I interpret the 'secret' to '*Think and Grow Rich*' to be that 'Rich' means life's riches, the money will take care of itself. Not everyone wants to be a millionaire and success means something different to everyone. Success for me is to become a recognized photographer producing work that inspires others and having happy children with goals and ambitions of their own. Whatever 'success' means to you, in this book lays the way to your own personal achievements. No doubt the 'secret' is also in the use of *all* these principles together. It is no good just reading the book and expecting the book to change your life. That is like joining the gym and expecting the membership to get you fit. You must put all the lessons into action to reach your true potential.

I first came across the works of Napoleon Hill in a piece of junk mail ten years ago. A bright red booklet in a clear plastic cover arrived through my letterbox. In bold yellow and white text it read 'Achieve the Impossible, Break Through To An Extraordinary and Fulfilling Life.' I still have it. The booklet arrived at a time when I was about to visit my doctor for anti-depressant pills.

I had three young children, a husband who worked constantly and I was a full time mum drowning in domesticity. Life seemed very bleak; I was very lonely and very lost. My only goal was to find 'me' again. That would be fulfilling enough. Acting on the lessons in this book introduced 'me' to 'me.' My first reading of the book inspired a more positive mental attitude to deal with my life as it was. Once I had made substantial changes to my everyday life I felt the need to really put these principles to the test. The next piece of junk mail to arrive read, 'Mystery, Exhilaration, Adventure—Make The Choice, Make a Difference—raise money for disadvantaged children and hike 60km to Machu Picchu.' I knew immediately that this was how I was meant to test the Napoleon Hill principles. Using all the wisdom and advice from Napoleon Hill I went on to raise £4000 (over $6000) for charity and hike 60km at high altitude through the Andes to Machu Picchu with forty strangers. To achieve this goal, every principle came into play starting with my 'burning desire' of getting to Machu Picchu. To raise the funds I had to step way out of my comfort zone. I used my 'sub-conscious mind' to visualize myself making presentations in front of hundreds of people to raise the funds. I created my 'mastermind group' of close friends and family to support me through the doubting days and to celebrate my success. My children were key players in my 'mastermind group'; we made endless amounts of cakes to sell and made a fund raising thermometer for the wall. They proudly took turns in colouring in the money raised each day. We set financial goals, created a plan and achieved them. Perhaps Napoleon Hill's secret in the book is to **think** of your goal and then get into **action** with total belief in your vision!

September 23rd 2001 was the day we set off on the hike; it was also my daughter's 9th birthday. She let me go with her blessing. I was excited and sick with nerves, not knowing what to expect. I didn't know anyone on the expedition, but this didn't last very long. I had found my old self. I was back. Napoleon Hill's 'Science of Personal Achievement' really did work.

When the new 'me' arrived home my life had to be different. I had made fundamental changes inside of me and I would not allow myself to sink back to that previous low. With all the strength that I had gained from putting the Napoleon Hill principles into practice through both reading and the online study course, I stepped out to get a degree in Photography. This was something that I should have done at the age of 24 and I was now 37. I had a great 'mastermind group' for encouragement when times got tough and a support team of family and friends to cover childcare. My desire was truly a burning one as I burned the midnight oil on a regular basis writing essays and putting work together. Napoleon Hill not only changed my life but also saved it. I was not yet financially rich but my life was getting richer by the day from a more positive outlook with the children and all the new, lovely, mind stretching information I was absorbing from the degree. Three years later my achievement was accomplished and for the last five years I have worked freelance throughout the United Kingdom as a Commercial and Fine Art Photographer.

Unfortunately, when you make spiritual changes, long-term internal changes, and practice the Napoleon Hill principles change will take place. Sometimes, only sometimes, you no longer fit the world you previously created and some years later my marriage gave way.

'... all who succeed in life get off to a bad start, and pass through many heartbreaking struggles before they 'arrive.' The turning point of those who succeed usually comes at the moment of some crisis, through which they are introduced to their other selves.' P27 Think and Grow Rich

After my separation I found myself with the love of my life. The true me, the new me had attracted her soul mate. I was very happy. He was wonderful to me, kind, loving, protective and funny. Our lives were challenging but I believed we were together forever. Nothing could break the love we had for each other. I believed that true love could conquer all. Unfortunately, whilst writing this chapter I had no idea that 'the rug' was going to be drastically pulled from under my feet by the 'love of my life' (so far)! I had no idea that I was about to be knocked down by a big emotional steamroller. My life with him was immediately over as he had found someone else. Once the shock had subsided sufficiently for me to think straight, I realized that, once again, in fact even more than before, I needed to draw on Napoleon Hill's 'success principles.' I knew from past experience that the 'Think and Grow Rich' approach worked, so it was time to 'think' myself out of this situation and find new riches in my life. We are what we think and we have two options, positive or negative. Negative thinking is just not an option when you believe in the works of Napoleon Hill.

'Strange and varied are the ways of life, and stranger still are the ways of infinite intelligence.' P28 Think and Grow Rich

Infinite Intelligence is a remarkable and perfect thing even if it is a big kick up the backside with a steel capped size eleven boot! Immediately I could see the reason for being asked to contribute to this book and contributing the photography has been my saving grace, the light at the end of my tunnel. Had I not had the experience of practicing the Napoleon Hill Principles, I probably would not have seen this as an opportunity, rather something that was too challenging while coping with a broken heart. However, these principles were now a part of me and I could see the opportunity and I grasped it immediately. Suddenly, I had a new 'Definiteness of Purpose' staring me in the face. All I had to do was pick myself up, dust myself down, forgive the actions of my previous lover and offer thanks to 'infinite intelligence' for the divine timing of this opportunity. Not easy when you feel like someone has just stuck a knife in your gut and turned it around several times. However, even at my lowest ebb I knew that it was up to me to pull the knife out. It was up to me how long I held onto the pain. Now more than ever it was essential for me to have a 'positive mental attitude,' not only for my own success but also for the love of my children. Life is short and I didn't want to waste a moment in getting over this. Napoleon Hill reminds us to look for the seed of an equivalent benefit in every defeat experienced; he also recommends that the best time to start looking for that seed in a new defeat is NOW.

Work would be my salvation. I decided to have some alone time and headed to Cornwall for a week, to the wonderful energy of the sea. I decided to camp so that I was forced to be alone. I intended to go for images for this project but healing turned out to be the reason. It was time to use my subconscious mind and take control of this pain by praying and meditating. I realized that my mind was filled with negative emotions, jealousy, hatred, anger but most of all the fear of not loving again. The fear of loneliness. 'The only thing to fear is fear itself.' It was time to get a hold of this and leave it behind in order to open myself up to new opportunities. Fear will never reveal new opportunities. They won't be visible.

The fear of the loss of love of someone is the most painful of all the six basic fears. It probably plays more havoc with the body and mind than any of the others. P271 Think and Grow Rich

When the feelings of jealousy, anger and disappointment are consuming your mind, nasty chemicals penetrate your blood and it feels like acid burning you up inside. I would shake, feel sick, not eat. I couldn't eat. In meditation, either in my tent or while walking the coastal path in the pouring rain (it is England after all!) alone, I would focus on replacing these negative emotions with love, peace and acceptance. I visualized forgiving this man and releasing him with love to go and be happy in the path that he had chosen. I would do this in the middle of the night when the jealousy and anger started to consume me again, all the while focussing on the positive outcome of my own success, seeing myself happy and laughing once again. I had to do this many times and sometimes I still have to do it.

Nothing in this world can take the place of persistence. Talent will not; nothing is more common than unsuccessful people with talent.
Genius will not; unrewarded genius is almost a proverb.
Education will not; the world is full of educated derelicts.
Persistence and determination are omnipotent.
                                        Calvin Coolidge (1872–1933)

Persistence plays a massive part in all success. I live in a valley in the Pennine Hills of Yorkshire, England. I start my day at 6 am with a 3-mile walk to meditate and set goals for the day to achieve the successful life I desire. I walk at speed, shoulders back, head held high. A confident walk builds confidence on the inside. Starting the day this way is also a great way to keep my 'positive mental attitude' in check. When the weather is dark and wet, this is the time when it is most challenging but it is also the time when I return home most invigorated and enthusiastic. I remind myself that when the going gets tough the tough get going! With the images from this book I now have a great source of reference to inspire and motivate people around the world but that is only part of the success.

'*Riches do not respond to wishes. They respond only to definite plans, backed by definite desires, through constant persistence.*' P187
Think and Grow Rich

It is now essential for me to develop 'persistence' in the ways that Napoleon Hill suggests in his book and make it a habit. Only when these principles become a habit can they serve you well. The habit of persistence will lead you to freedom of thought and independence and will guarantee favourable 'breaks.' It is the habit that will turn dreams into reality. As Calvin Coolidge reminds us, persistence and determination are everything.

This personal defeat has given me great strengths in many ways. Previously I suffered from 'fear of criticism.' I was afraid to put my work out for all to see. My smaller self didn't really believe my work was creative enough or good enough to succeed in this very competitive field. Who am I to think that people will want to publish my work when there are already so many amazing photographers? I now feel that no one can hurt me more than I have just been hurt and I have survived that, so this gives me a certain amount of confidence to put my goals into action.

You must first burn down the forest for new roots to grow.

Recently, I have produced stronger and bolder images. My fearless creativity is being developed. So long as I believe in the images I am producing and have the vision for where I want them to go and act on my plan for their success, with persistence I believe I will achieve the success I am aiming for. It is time to stop hiding my light under a bushel.

'To get ahead you first have to stick your neck out.'
—W. Clement Stone

I have always dreamed of having my work published in a book. Working with the Napoleon Hill Foundation has been my first opportunity and I am sure there are more books inside me waiting to come out. In the meantime, it is my intention that these powerful images that capture each chapter of Napoleon Hill's work at a glance will be exhibited and sold worldwide so that they can inspire and motivate people. Napoleon Hill produced his work during the depression in the 1930's and his work made a major contribution to turning the American economy around by changing the way people think. The world is once again at an economic low and inspiration is what is needed. I am flattered that my work will make a contribution in some way and that it stands alongside such a great man who still inspires long after he has passed away.

'Transmutation of sex energy calls for more will power than the average person cares to use for this purpose' however, *'the reward for the practice is more than worth the effort.'* P.220 Think and Grow Rich

The 'Sex Transmutation' principle made me feel down, initially, as I interpreted it that I would have to give up my sex/love life if I desired to be successful. 'Sex Transmutation' is not about denying your sexuality and suppressing your libido, quite the opposite, this principle is about harnessing sexual feelings. It is about feeling sexual energy every day in order to feel inspired with your desired goal. When we are sexually attracted to a partner we feel alive, energetic, positive, inspired. We can feel it spilling out of us and we inspire others with our enthusiasm for life. We love everything, from the birds in the trees to the postman! We sing more, we dance more and we smile more. 'Sex Transmutation' is the success habit that will harness this energy for your own desire. It is essential to identify how we create this energy and keep it for ourselves so that it can be transmuted to our own personal passion. Whether that is art, literature, photography, work or simply being happy with our health and wellbeing. Energy breeds energy. Learn to capture the most powerful and influential energy and there will be some left over to share with a partner. This will also be authentic energy and long lasting because it will come from within rather than being dependent on the lover in your life.

'*The emotion of sex is a virtue only when used intelligently and with discrimination. It may often be misused to such an extent that it debases, instead of enriches, both body and mind.*' P.220 Think and Grow Rich

Sexual energy is dangerous when it is dependent on a reaction to the love of another, as we tend to throw all our eggs in one basket. To experience the joy of sexual energy and then have it taken away can cause serious depression and lead people to act uncharacteristically. Learning to harness this within yourself and for yourself can act as an antidepressant. I have learned that you must *never* give all of your sexual energy away, that way no one has the power to pull the rug from under your feet and break your heart. You may miss someone for a while but your heart and soul will still be yours and in tact.

To be successful at the 'Sex Transmutation principle' you must express it every day. Dress well, eat well and avoid fatty foods and alcohol and have a daily exercise routine. All of this will produce enough Serotonin to keep the spring in your step and turn that energy into genius. Napoleon Hill describes it as alchemy, turning something basic into gold! Express sexual energy in your body language, your tone of voice and every-thing about you. Successful people are full of charm and cha-risma; this is sexual energy that is transmuted to success. Keep it and use it properly.

'The energy must be transmuted from desire of physical contact into some other form of desire and action before it will lift one to the status of genius.' P.216 Think and Grow Rich

A successful career is an essential part of the fulfillment of my life. As painful as this part of my life has been it has proven to be an opportunity to channel this energy and focus completely on the creativity required for my work. It has also allowed me to focus on what my values are and to live by them through both business and family. The long-term 'benefits of success' and 'personal fulfillment' far outweigh the instant gratification of sex and is worth the effort for the long term.

'If you can conceive and believe it, you can achieve it.'
—Napoleon Hill

To achieve, to step up above the majority, you need to believe in your vision, yourself and in the universe to take you along the correct path. The 'secret' that Napoleon Hill writes about on every page of his book is in the title. The book 'Think and Grow Rich' is a strong message in belief and action. Belief is the 'Think' part of the title and 'Growth' is the action. In every case study he discusses, using all his wisdom of the principles that he has identified, he can't stress enough the importance to believe AND GET INTO ACTION STRAIGHT AWAY, EVEN IF YOU DON'T FEEL YOU ARE READY. The secret on every page of his book has to be 'if you can believe it, you can achieve it.' Belief in vision and action creates massive changes in the world, from wars to the invention of the Internet! If belief and action can be that powerful then we must learn to believe in our vision and create a plan to manifest what we see in our heart and mind. Napoleon Hill identified thirteen principles of success that are all based on the 'belief' of success. When I agreed to do the photography project for this book I had no idea HOW I was going to achieve finding or creating the images. I just BELIEVED in the vision of the final images and that I would, without any doubt, achieve this. So I WENT TO WORK IMMEDIATELY. The images from that belief and action now illustrate Napoleon Hill's principles in this book. I am sure they will inspire people all around the world, just like the text from Napoleon Hill's life long work in *Think and Grow Rich*.

"Vision without action is just a dream.
Action without vision is simply passing the time.
Action with vision can change the world."
Joel Barker

Special thanks to Joel Barker for the use of his inspiring quote.

About Janet Jones

Janet Jones is a professionally qualified photographer based in York-shire, England. She specializes in Commercial and Fine Art photography and her work can be seen on many websites and in business exhibitions. Janet is also a certified Napoleon Hill Instructor and she incorporates the 'Success Principles' into her life daily. You can reach Janet via her website at www.janetjonesphotography.co.uk.

15

The Secret for Everyone

by Kathleen Betts
TORONTO, CANADA

"It is one of the most beautiful compensations
in life that no man can sincerely try to help
another without helping himself."

—RALPH WALDO EMERSON

As seekers of success and happiness, many of us have had
the good fortune to stumble on Dr. Napoleon Hill's lifework
or to have it shared with us by someone we knew who learned
and profited from the philosophy and instructions he outlined
in his flagship book, *Think and Grow Rich*. Dr. Hill invitingly
scattered clues throughout the chapters and assured us that,
"Somewhere, as you read, the secret to which I refer will jump
from the page and stand boldly before you, IF YOU ARE
READY FOR IT! When it appears, you will recognize it.
Whether you receive the sign in the first or the last chapter,
stop for a moment when it presents itself, and turn down a
glass, for that occasion will mark the most important turning-

point of your life." If this eye-opening moment is so momentous as to justly cause pause for thought as the life-altering revelation Dr. Hill touts it to be, how can some of us read all the way through the book, possibly more than once, and still not have it jump out at us?

As an enthusiast of Dr. Hill's lifework, this writer is honored to contribute to these testimonials with ardent hope of helping readers find their answer. Having thought I saw the secret first on page 40 of my copy, in the words "by giving before they try to get," I finally pronounced a celebratory "Aha!" and I turned down my glass at page 115, when I read "giving in return an equivalent value of one form or another." What I had been looking for appeared to jump off the page. If uncovering the secret could be done by simply referring others to the pages where we found it, there would be no purpose or substance for the book you have in hand. Dr. Hill's instructions helped me clarify my objective and espouse the principles vital to achieving it. It was when my own idea of what exactly I wanted to have and to do became clear to me that I was able to understand and see what Dr. Hill's secret was.

As cosmic habit force, I begin any discussion on success with my primary achievement of being the luckiest mother in the world to my four precious children and hoping that all other parents share the same sense for themselves. Another extraordinary achievement I wouldn't miss incorporating in this discussion is that of having this chance and honor to hopefully inspire others who are on their journey to succeed. It has become one of my greatest passions to share Dr. Hill's philosophy, especially with those who are ready to *Think and Grow Rich*, or are preparing to be ready, as is presumably the case with readers of this very material. I am ever grateful for your interest and hopeful that what you're reading will permit you to turn down your glass soon too in recognition of marking the most important turning-point in your life.

Piquing our eager curiosity, in his introductory pages, Dr. Hill stated "The secret to which I refer has been mentioned no fewer than a hundred times throughout this book." With the answer before us no fewer than one hundred times, surely finding it should be easier than the needle-in-the-haystack search it feels like as we pore over every word with anticipation. Dr. Hill further counseled: "It has not been directly named, for it seems to work more successfully when it is merely uncovered and left in sight, where those who are ready, and searching for it, may pick it up." Through the course of our read-to-reap-fortune venture, at times, we suppose we have cracked the mystery only to find it either zaps or fades slowly from the catch of our mind's eye. The "secret" can seem to be an enigma-wrapped-in-a-puzzle conundrum. Maybe what's happening is a subconscious lost-in-the-woods feeling is leaving us unable to see the trees for the forest.

Ironically, the secret is so obvious, our grasp of it can be tenuous because of a that-can't-really-be-all-there-is-to-it skepticism we summon when we have flickering thoughts of "maybe that's it." Some of the perplexity is attributable to the term "secret." If instead of calling it a secret, we called it "what is blatantly obvious," we may find it easier to understand. Our very thoughts create the shroud we think up in our minds by calling it a secret. One of the clues that Dr. Hill offered in the "Imagination" chapter was that, "Strange and paradoxical as it may seem, the 'secret' is not a secret." He further counseled in his next paragraph: "Above all, do not stop, nor hesitate in your study of these principles until you have read the book at least three times, for then, you will not want to stop."

Paradoxically or intrinsically, our challenge in conclusively seizing the secret is conjoined to the constantly changing ideas, thoughts and beliefs that pass through our minds. Adding to the complexity is the combined element of our personal experiences, burning desires, goals, objectives, dreams, and temporary defeats all being inextricably linked to what we believe qualifies as or defines success. These constantly changing factors create a moving target effect with the result of our stronghold on the "secret" waxing and waning. This morphing in our minds, as it turns out, is a robust clue. Once we have a clear picture in our minds of a static objective and a lucid personal definition of success, we are more likely ready to see the secret jump from the pages.

It's helpful to consider tips from other greats who either influenced or were influenced by Dr. Hill. One of particular note and unmatched in his eloquence, was Ralph Waldo Emerson who penned countless insightful and inspiring essays and poems on the subject.

What is Success?
　　To laugh often and much;
　　To win the respect of intelligent people
　　　　and the affection of children;
　　To earn the appreciation of honest critics
　　　　and endure the betrayal of false friends;
　　To appreciate beauty;
　　To find the best in others;
　　To leave the world a bit better,
　　　　whether by a child,
　　　　a garden patch,
　　　　or a redeemed social condition;
　　To know even one life has breathed easier because you
　　　　have lived.
　　This is to have succeeded.

Earl Nightingale told us "Success is the progressive realization of a worthy goal. Or in some cases the pursuit of a
worthy ideal." His definition leads us to understand that anyone who's on course toward the fulfillment of a goal is already
enjoying success, if they will allow themselves the liberty to
accept the concept. Reinforcing his definition, Mr. Nightingale elaborated, "Now, success doesn't lie in the achievement
of a goal, although that's what the world considers success; it
lies in the journey toward the goal. We're successful as long
as we're working toward something we want to bring about in
our lives. That's when the human being is at his or her best.
That's what Cervantes meant when he wrote, 'The road is
better than the inn.' We're at our best when we're climbing,
thinking, planning, working. When we're on the road toward
something we want to bring about."

More recently, Jack Canfield tells us that "Life is not about
achievement, it's about learning and growth, and developing
qualities like compassion, patience, perseverance, love, and joy,
and so forth." Consider that "learning and growth, and developing qualities like compassion, patience, perseverance, love,
and joy" are at once achievements in and of themselves while
also being the means to other ends of more tangible or measurable goals. What a wonderful world to live in if in years to
come, we could all make that stretch.

Recalling that success is subjective wherein what one
considers meager, another considers opulent, what we're
really after here is the secret to what most of us consider to
be extraordinary success. It's worth noting nonetheless that
giving ourselves credit for these salt-of-the-earth simpler successes puts us in good stead to be ready for extraordinary
success. The secret of success of any magnitude is what one
believes it to be. The complexity stems from the simplicity. It

only seems difficult to grasp because we think there must be more to it. I would suggest that the evasiveness of what we think we should easily see emanates from within each one of us. It's personal and subjective to a much greater degree than it is objective. What the secret is may differ as much for each of us as the point in time of reading at which our "aha moment of thought" might occur to us. Studying one of the targets, by clarifying in our minds what success means to us and accepting that it is a process and not a destination, makes it easier to think our way through what the secret is. Burning desire was a key that Dr. Hill repeated emphatically. In setting the goals we will use to measure our success, we have to think in terms of our true burning desires.

As a point to ponder on burning desire, I recall a day about twenty years ago when I was visiting with friends and ogling over luxurious boats at a yacht club in British Columbia. One had a particular allure for me and I snapped a shot of it, thinking when I'm ready for a boat, that's the one I want. I've often thought about that boat over the years and felt a little twinge of disappointment in myself over not having met my goal to acquire it. It dawned on me one day that mingled in with that sense of disappointment were some other stronger sentiments like "What would I do with it? Where would we keep it? How often would we get a chance to use it? How much does a boat like that pollute the environment?"

I still love boats and anything that gets me closer to the water and don't begrudge anyone else the enjoyment they get from theirs. What a relief it was though one day when I realized my sense of disappointment at not having the boat was so irrational. I had never had a true burning desire to have that boat. It was more of a mixture of emotions wherein the doubtful thoughts I had actually outweighed my desire to have the boat. I relate this experience now as the realization serves as a useful tool for me and I hope it will for others too in differentiating between true burning desires with associated goals and whims of fancy based on what might popularly be considered a symbol of success.

There's no measure of failure in not owning a yacht for anyone who doesn't have a burning desire to own a yacht. Does that make sense? It works with anything you can think of. It doesn't have to be a yacht. It can be a career or professional objective, a financial goal, a relationship, material possessions, etc. . . . It's likely we have less trouble figuring out what the secret is and more trouble figuring out what our goals are and what metrics to use to measure our success.

Dr. Hill instructed us to attune ourselves to our truest desires and to rigorously incorporate the principles he developed to help us find ways to turn our thoughts into reality. All of the elements of the philosophy are entwined to each other and end up having an inter-dependence or reinforcing effect on each other. While it may be far-fetched to expect that commonly they can all be mastered, it is evident in the analysis of those who have achieved remarkable success, omitting any one of them even temporarily will weaken our endeavors. Focusing on some more than others is not the same as omitting any. It's natural and advisable to gravitate to the principles that come more easily to us. There is a trick though to not letting those that require more effort go by the wayside entirely. Dr. Hill provided us examples of how the individuals he researched over the years had different strengths and adhered more strictly to some principles than others.

The principles that resonate most with me are those in the category of personal integrity, including the golden rule. Part of the secret to success is to figure out which elements of the principles resonate most with individual characters and goals. One of the examples of extraordinary successes that Dr. Hill referenced was the story of Arthur Nash, a tailor from Cincinnati who used his nearly bankrupt business to test the success formula. Having researched Mr. Nash myself in preparing this chapter, I was astonished to find how salient the message was of his clear understanding of the secret as I see it. Anyone looking for ideas or inspiration to help them uncover the secret might find it useful to study his story.

Once we have our clear idea of what our goals are, we must pursue them relentlessly without compromising our morals or integrity, always with consideration to the impact our actions and decisions will have on others affected by our words and our thoughts or by what we do or what we fail to do. By weighing our decisions on a scale of "What's in it for everyone?" we find the guidance we need to stay the course of integrity in all our transactions. When we meet goals resulting in net gains for all who are effected, our success is multiplied exponentially. It makes perfect sense by business and or humanitarian standards. The more people are served by our goals, the more likely we are to succeed. If we compromise integrity or ideals or if the adverse effects of any steps one takes to achieve his or her goals outweigh the overall benefits, then failure rather than success is what the attainment of those riches amounts to. When we predicate our actions and decisions on the inspiration and driving force of the fifth element of Napoleon Hill's Self-Confidence Formula, we are guided to progress toward our goals in manners that are reflective of the composite of principles Dr. Hill promoted as necessary constituents to the secret of success. The powerful message enveloped in his words can be used as a personal barometer, compass, map, communicator and propeller all wrapped up in one handy implement more versatile than the most recent electronic gadgetry of the day.

For those who don't have it committed to memory, the wording is as follows:

"I fully realize that no wealth or position will long endure, unless built upon truth and justice; therefore, I will engage in no transaction that does not benefit all whom it affects. I will succeed by attracting to myself the forces I wish to use and the cooperation of other people. I will induce others to serve me because of my willingness to serve others. I will eliminate hatred, envy, jealousy, selfishness, and cynicism, by developing love for all humanity, because I know that a negative attitude toward others can never bring me success."

Following Dr. Hill's prescription for success does not mean that we will not encounter obstacles along the way. Having challenges and adversities in our life of course does not equate to failure. In his book entitled *Set Yourself on Fire*, Phil Taylor who is my dear friend and an emerging force in the field of self-development, included a chapter on "The Gift of Adversity." In his words, "I look back and delight in my difficulties, for they have been my teachers, and have been the very motivation that spurs me forward in the pursuit of these two life-enhancing principles." If we are looking for seeds of opportunity in our challenges, our prospects for success are enhanced. Considering every adversity carries with it a seed of equal or greater opportunity, instead of lamenting we should be clicking our heels to the count of our blessings when we react to our challenges. What goes wrong is the kick-start to almost all the products and services that have turned lucrative dividends for those who react by seizing the opportunity to find a solution through a "what's-in-it-for-everyone?" mentality. That's not to say either that it's easy to overcome every challenge we'll meet.

As early readers, we may have learned from Dr. Seuss in *Oh the Places You'll Go*, that there will be slumps we'll have to go through. We then have to find the courage and conviction to do what Dr. Seuss brilliantly termed "unslumping ourselves." As an aside, that might well be the most useful information the good fortune of contributing to this book will allow me to share with readers, Dr. Seuss is an exceptional motivator who clearly must have grasped Dr. Hill's secret. The tremendous collection of children's stories he created reminds me of the lessons from Malcolm Hillgartner and Robert Fulghum who both have inspired us to think about how all and everything we need to know, we learned in Kindergarten. Not to slight the value of commitment to lifelong learning, those early years set the foundation for our success.

Thinking back to how to get "unslumped," when you take everything you have in life and put it on a scale, if what you love and wouldn't change for the world outweighs what needs improvement, count those blessings as successes and draw from that powerful place the strength to get out of the rut and back on the path to achieving goals. If the scale tips the other way, it will require even greater effort and would be a good idea to draw strength from the examples of others. An element of the secret is that we are all successful until we quit. We are learning from our adversities and finding in them the opportunities that exist to make the world a better place for ourselves and for others.

We can still live the dreams we envisioned even when some days don't go the way we would like them to. We're exactly where we are as a result of the complement of decisions we've made along the way. By choosing to surround ourselves with people we admire and who inspire us to want to improve ourselves, we fortify our means to progress toward our goals. We have to surround ourselves with sufficient positive influence to make a greater impact on us than whatever negative influences might be in our midst. By dosing ourselves with a daily fortifier of inspiration, we can find the strength we need to propel ourselves toward our goals and not only ward off negative influences but equip ourselves to instead have a positive influence on others who will likely appreciate the leadership. If in good conscience we can look in the mirror and smile at that person with pride, we're on the right path to finding the secret and to whatever extraordinary success we truly believe we can achieve.

Truth be known, the secret might appear before us on any page in the book because it resides in our own thoughts and ideas, to be projected onto something before our eyes. There is definitely an increased likelihood that the realization will "jump out" at us while we're reading *Think and Grow Rich* because Dr. Hill's systematized principles are an excellent tool to evoke whatsoever we believe to be the secret and howsoever we define success, both of which come from within each one of us. Once the idea crystallizes in our minds, success is inevitable when we adhere to the principles. The secret is in keeping the idea crystal clear and maintaining the personal rigor and constitution it requires to consistently adhere to the principles.

Reading *Think and Grow Rich* at least three times, as suggested by the author, helps us to open our minds sufficiently and establish or instill in ourselves the habits and strength of conviction we need to relentlessly pursue success. By immersing our mental attitude in positive influences, adhering to the credo that "A quitter never wins and a winner never quits" and committing ourselves to lifelong engagement to transactions that benefit all whom they affect, the so-called secret to success will become so naturally unshrouded, we'll be left wondering instead how we could ever have thought there were any obstacles that were not in fact stepping stones to the extraordinary successes we see in the achievements of others we admire. In what we do to try to make the world better for everyone, we can't help but to make it better for ourselves too.

The very essence of success is the relentless pursuit of it. So to speak, we have to let success go to our heads, although not in the figurative sense. Perhaps more accurately, we have to let it come from our heads in the form of ideas we believe will be helpful to the world we live in. After all, as Dr. Hill mentioned in some words or another in every chapter of *Think and Grow Rich*, "Whatever the mind can conceive, and believe, it can achieve." It's beautiful. Shall we turn down a glass?

About Kathleen Betts

Kathleen Betts sits on the Board of Directors for the not-for-profit newspaper, Good News Toronto. As a freelancer and blogger she has a mission to share stories that inspire integrity and motivate goodwill toward others. She lives in Scarborough, Canada with her husband Mike and their four precious children, with a commitment to help them and other young learners, as well as adults who are ready, to embrace and benefit from Napoleon Hill's philosophy. Contact Kathleen through the GNT website at www.goodnewstoronto.ca or at tripsr4kids@rogers.com.

16

What is the secret in Think and Grow Rich?

by Rajiv Mathews George, PCC, CPC
KUALA LUMPUR, MALAYSIA

"In a time of drastic change it is the learners who inherit the future. The learned usually find themselves equipped to live in a world that no longer exists. "
–ERIC HOFFER

I was attracted to read *Think and Grow Rich* when I saw it available all over India. At first, I thought it was a marketing gimmick to make the author rich.

After 12 years of studying and working in the United States, I concluded my life story in one simple sentence, "The Rise & Fall of Rajiv Mathews—The Water Tiger." I have lost everything in life—my personal wealth and belongings, my wife left. I was family-less, money-less and homeless.

The turning point struck when I was invited to attend a preview by Napoleon Hill Associates (NHA), Malaysia in

2003. I invested on The Habitizing Programme for 12 weeks, Science of Success for 6 months (PMA Science of Success), NHA Trainer Certification, *Think and Grow Rich* Certification at NHA, Kuala Lumpur.

My great achievement of reading *Think and Grow Rich* for 30 times within ten years has attracted the 12 Riches and the transformation has been happening to me since 2001. Mr. Joe Dudley, Sr. who I met at Napoleon Hill International Convention has read *Think and Grow Rich* 300 times. My dream in 2010 came true when I was among the top 10 coaches in Malaysia. I was the fourth coach in Malaysia to be credentialed by ICF, the largest authority in professional coaching in the world. My business has grown through an active referral system.

Transformation happens to my coachees, students and participants but mostly to myself. Now, I support my mother happily, travel globally, taste delicious cuisine and stay healthy. I am also surrounded with many good networks. I have successfully managed 'the state of my mind' and continued to focus on my big dreams, followed my successful formula to change my and everyone's life to be better. The greatest gift is to live peacefully and happily in every moment to the fullest. I sincerely owe my gratitude to Dr. Hill, The Napoleon Hill Foundation and Napoleon Hill Associates.

Since 2001, I am proud to be a Managing Director of Harvest Global Resources Sdn. Bhd & Empower Coach Concepts who specializes in Sales Performance Coaching and Inner Game Coaching. In 2004, I discovered my Definite Major Purpose and realized my calling to empower people through coaching. I am from the first batch of Certified Coaches in Malaysia, recognized by International Coach Federation.

I believe through sharing, I will receive more.

There are few applications of the code of SECRET to be remembered as in the following:

1. You are the most important person in this world. You must BELIEVE YOURSELF to be able to move forward.
2. You are unique and your life is exclusively designed to succeed. You may apply your own formula to succeed.
3. Travel along an enjoyable journey to be successful. There isn't any shortcut. Success is a journey and not a destination.
4. Nothing is going to happen unless you take action. **No Action, No Success!**

If you have a new goal, you need to read *Think and Grow Rich* to reveal a different approach to succeed in your goal. Your goal might be looking for a new job, starting a new business, changing your life direction, recovering from a health issue, working on a new project, getting married, etc.

Think and Grow Rich has revealed the S.E.C.R.E.T to advance my life. They are the SEEDS for HARVESTING SUCCESS. Are you **READY** to apply it?

THE SECRET CODE IN THINK AND GROW RICH

© 2011 Rajiv Mathews

SELF-DISCIPLINE

ENTHUSIASM

CAPABILITY

RESPONSIBILITY

EDUCATION

THINKING

The above-mentioned tenets are connected. These are the results of applying the principles of success from Napoleon Hill's philosophy.

A. SELF DISCIPLINE

Napoleon Hill says it starts with the mastery of your thoughts.

Self Discipline is ultimately your development and enforcement of positive habits that you need to grow. There is not anyone who has not mastered self-discipline. Most people tend to be attracted to fun and easy activities. The person who possesses self-discipline embraces challenges for greater rewards. A classic example is Thomas Edison who invented the light bulb.

Key Performance Indicators of Self Discipline
Manage x Knowledge

My Experience:
My goal was to be a Certified Professional Coach. I committed time, effort and money to achieve my goal. I acquired *knowledge* and *managed* the information purposefully to be an effective coach. After five years in my Master Mind group, I am able to reinforce positive habits to be a Specialist in Sales Coaching.

Questions:
1. What knowledge are you seeking in the process of achieving your success?
2. What makes you a Specialist in your area of expertise?
3. How do you manage knowledge to achieve personal goals for a greater purpose?

B. ENTHUSIASM

Napoleon Hill says that Enthusiasm inspires action. It is the most contagious of all emotions.

Enthusiasm is faith in action. It is the intense emotion known as burning desire. Enthusiasm comes from within to radiate outwardly in the expression of one's voice and countenance. Enthusiasm is powerful when it is transmuted into action through faith.

The Flame of Enthusiasm is Burning Within You. Change your thoughts into action. This is Rajiv's lesson from Napoleon Hill.

Success Indicators of Enthusiasm
Interest x Action

My Experience:
There were not many coaches in 2000. I was committed to coach because it was my *interest* and calling in life. I learned and researched methods of coaching. I took deliberate *action* which included giving free 150 hours of complimentary coaching. My Coaching fees skyrocketed to more than 500% within three years.

Questions:
1. What career path are you interested in to fulfill your dreams?
2. What is your level of interest? (rate: 1 = low and 10 = high)?
3. What actions are you going to take to activate your interests?

C. CAPABILITY

Napoleon Hill says that capability comes from imagination. This is the one quality needed to combine specialized knowledge with IDEAS and organized plans to yield riches.

Success Indicators of Capability
Commitment x Desire

My Experience:

I have been *committed* relentlessly in designing and developing coaching programs for bringing awareness, building purpose, empowering the potential and bringing transformations in the lives of individuals since ten years ago. The outcome is able to develop ideas, techniques and processes to activate results. My business is solely built on referrals and has definitely attracted riches. My work was a reflection of my *desires* which brought fulfillment of completing a task and the people I worked with.

Questions:
1. What makes you committed towards your achievement?
2. What are the outcomes you want to achieve?
3. What do you do to practice your desires in daily work?

D. RESPONSIBILITY

Napoleon Hill says Big Pay and Little Responsibility are seldom found together. He says great achievement is usually born of great sacrifice, and is not the result of selfishness. Everybody wants something for nothing, but unfortunately life doesn't work that way. Great achievement requires great labour and great sacrifice.

Success Indicators of Responsibility
Manage x Fulfillment

My Experience:
One of the things that I focused on is *managing* my thoughts, my choices and my beliefs in the direction of my goals and purpose on a day-to-day basis (baby steps take you to giant leaps). Time management and choices of people you want to work with becomes absolutely important. I have managed time and people towards my areas of development, specialization and fulfillment. I always shift my focus from "What I do not want" to "What I want." I focus on solutions rather than on problems. I continue to strive for better value and happiness for my clients and friends.

Questions:
1. What are you going to do to manage your time, choices and people towards your goals and fulfillment?
2. What makes you happy? How do you apply it in your daily life?
3. What changes do you need to make to become more effective in your management and fulfillment?

E. EDUCATION
Napoleon Hill states that Education comes from within yourself. You must struggle and put more effort and thought into the process. The man who organizes and directs a Master Mind group of men who processes knowledge useful in the accumulation of money, is just as much a man of education, is just as much a man in the group.

Thomas A. Edison only had three months of formal schooling during his entire lifetime. But, he neither lacked education nor was he poor.

Success Indicators of Education
Awareness x Action

My Experience:
Change begins with *awareness and not education. Your* effort is to find what led to your disappointments and losses, i.e., your self-limiting beliefs. Being a member of my Master Mind group for 5 years has reframed my self-defeating beliefs. It involves taking mindless *actions,* initiative in MMA leadership, running projects, etc. We have been putting effort, time and money for continuous learning in selected books. The outcome is fantastic. I am attracted to the riches.

Questions:
1. What do you need to do for further education?
2. What are your fears? How are you going to resolve it?
3. What has stopped you from taking action? What do you need to do to change?

F. THINKING
Napoleon Hill says that "We are what we are, because of the vibrations of thought which we pick up and register, through the stimuli of our daily environment."

"We become what we think about all day long," according to Earl Nightingale.

Success Indicators of Thinking
Belief x Awareness

My Experience:

Through my experience, the power of questioning has moved me forward. It was important to challenge my *beliefs* and continue to purify my thoughts to build my awareness. The main purpose of reading *Think and Grow Rich* was not the book itself, however it was about purifying the thoughts in the process to attract riches. It can only 'be' with *Purpose, Process and Practice (3 P's) in everything you do.* This is the greatest secret for me.

Questions:
1. What are your challenging beliefs after reading *Think and Grow Rich?*
2. How do you plan to reframe your thoughts?
3. What do you think daily in relation to what you want to achieve?

About Rajiv Mathews George

Rajiv Mathews George is the Chief Listening Officer for Harvest Global Resources Sdn.Bhd based in Kuala Lumpur, Malaysia and he specializes in Sales Coaching. He is a Professional Certified Coach (PCC) with International Coach Federation (ICF) and a Certified Trainer with Napoleon Hill Associates, Malaysia, and he can he reached at rajiv.mathews@harvestglobalresources.com.

There is a difference between wishing for a thing and being ready to receive it. No one is ready for a thing until he believes he can acquire it. The state of mind must be belief, not mere hope or wish. Open-mindedness is essential for belief. Closed minds do not inspire faith, courage, and belief.

—NAPOLEON HILL

17

Napoleon Hill's Secret

by John A. Cramer
HOUSTON, TEXAS

I. INTRODUCTION

Over twenty years have gone by since I first read Napoleon Hill's, *Think and Grow Rich*. And throughout that time, my understanding of the secret has continued to evolve and change. The journey for me has been more like a game of cat and mouse. Just as I was sure I discovered what the secret was, it would invariably lead me someplace else where I would again land on what I thought to be "it"!

At times, I would struggle and get confused. Maybe I tried too hard to find it. Maybe I just wasn't ready to see it. Often frustration and anger would follow. At one point I considered there might not be a secret at all, just a joke Hill played on his readers. But, I never lost faith in wanting to find the secret. Although I had already achieved some measure of success in my career and personal life, I knew deep down inside I was capable of achieving more.

II. "PAST" SECRETS

Initially, I thought that the secret was about desire and the unwillingness to recognize failure. In the second chapter of his book, Hill provides a six step process to "turn desire into gold." This resonated with me. I had already applied the process quite successfully early in my career before I even became aware of it and had achieved astonishing results.

For a while I focused on avoiding the thirty-one major causes of failure. These "Golden Rules" provided me the structure and discipline I needed to become more efficient in manifesting my goals. Following that, I entered a new level of awareness, thinking that the secret was really about the power of faith and autosuggestion. And, until recently, I was convinced the secret was about persistence.

Every time I "rediscovered" the secret, I had an "ah ha!" moment and knew this was it, *really*! It made sense for me at that moment in my life. And, in each of those moments, wonderful and amazing things would happen which reinforced and confirmed my understanding of the principles at play.

Recognizing this, I've recently come to a new realization: the secret reveals itself in the right form that matches one's ability to receive it. It's a Rorschach test. The secret is a reflection of what your mind is willing to accept. Hill said, "No one is ready for a thing until he believes he can acquire it." That goes for the secret as well. And, in my own experience, once I believed I could acquire it, it met me on my own terms and only to the degree I was willing to accept it.

III. WHAT IS THE SECRET FOR ME TODAY?

So what is the secret that Napoleon Hill talks about? All who have read the book are familiar with the tantalizing hints found in his introduction, that the secret comes in two parts, one of which is already in possession by those who are ready for it. Hill writes, "It has not been directly named, for it seems to work more successfully when it is merely uncovered and left in sight, where those who are ready, and searching for it, may pick it up."

Over the years, I've arrived at the simplest and most straight-forward understanding of the secret. In fact, Hill wasted no time in expressing the essence of it. The secret appears in the opening sentence of the first chapter of the book. "Truly, thoughts are things, and powerful things at that, when they are mixed with definiteness of purpose, persistence, and a burning desire for their translation into riches, or other material objects."

There are three quintessential components of the secret formula—thought, emotion, and action. The degree of success realized, or manifested in material form, is a function of multiple factors of all three components. They include the *clarity* and *detail* of the thought, the *power of one's belief* in that thought and its *alignment* to right purpose; the *intensity* of the attached emotion *expressed positively* and moving *toward the desired outcome*; and the *cumulative energy* of the action *performed by the individual* in pursuing the intended goal.

Thought, emotion, and action do not act independently of each other but coexist in an interconnected, cybernetic environment. Each has the ability to influence and be influenced by the other. Said another way, what we think influences what we feel and do. What we feel drives what we think and do. And, what we do drives what we think and feel. By focusing and changing one element, we can influence and change the other two. This allows us opportunities to apply the secret from three different aspects or states of mind. Those who "think" their way to success allow their thoughts to drive their feelings and actions. Those who "feel" their desires and dreams use their heart to drive thinking and action. And, those who act decisively in moving toward their goal will think and feel through their action.

What Hill's secret reveals is that by aligning thought, emotion, and action to one unified purpose, all three aspects triangulate to the pinpointed objective. The focused energy flowing toward it creates a magnetic pull which attracts and manifests the desired result.

Looking back on my life, I can see an arc in the development of my conscious awareness. I can point to experiences where each of these aspects dominated at different times, leading the other two toward a unified purpose. As a young man in my twenties, passion and emotion drove my thoughts and actions. In my thirties and early forties, I relied on action to guide my feelings. In my late forties, I focused on thoughts and beliefs, many of which were driving negative emotions and dysfunctional behavior. At fifty I had a spiritual awakening and recognized the power of faith and autosuggestion. Now, just three years later, my focus has shifted yet again, this time on optimizing the integration of all three aspects aligned within the context of right purpose.

The following are three examples from my life which illustrate how I applied the secret from various points in the progression of the arc. In each case, regardless which aspect led, once all three aligned with a unified purpose, I successfully achieved my goal. But first, a warning to the reader: beware what you ask for. As you will soon learn, success for me didn't necessarily guarantee happiness.

IV. DESIRE: WHEN PASSION RULED!

As far back as I can remember I've harbored a strong sense of wanderlust. In high school I dreamed of spending a year abroad as a foreign exchange student. My family had no money grow-ing up. Vacations to Europe were out of the question, much less the cost of spending a year abroad. As each year passed, the urge to leave home and go to Europe grew stronger. I could taste the anticipation of one day achieving my dream.

I learned to play the violin at an early age. It turned out, I actually had a talent for it and the violin served me well throughout my high school and college days. I got pretty good, at least good enough to win several competitions. I quickly earned the reputation of being a competent violinist and began performing professionally before I finished high school.

I freelanced in the evenings and on weekends playing in orchestras, wedding quartets and holiday music concerts. I got a job as a strolling violinist in a popular local band known as "The Gypsies." We played traditional folk, gypsy, and classi-cal music to dinner patrons at several upscale restaurants. We performed two to three nights a week strolling around dinner tables, dressed in costumes, and speaking in fake European accents. Nobody actually believed we were real gypsies, but we had lots of fun pretending and our antics made people smile and laugh. I got quite proficient dodging waiters with large serving trays, turning on the charm for patrons, improvising requested tunes, and extracting large tips. The job was a kick and financially rewarding. I got paid $50 a night plus tips. In the mid 70s, minimum wage was only $1.65 an hour. Earning $150–$200 a week was serious dough, and by the time I finished my freshman year in college, I had saved up enough money to buy a used car, attend an out of state university, and say good-bye to Houston.

I transferred to Illinois State University my sophomore year. Campus housing placed me in International House, a dormitory program designed for foreign students. I found it amusing that my "out of state" status would qualify me as a fit. Very quickly I realized the tremendous value of living in I-House. I met students from all over the world, got exposed to various cultures, and learned about their foods, history and social mores. These experiences further fueled my desire to travel. As a future "citizen of the world" I would need to know these things.

There was an exchange program with a university in Germany. Students invited to participate would have their tuition costs waived for a year as they attended classes abroad. I was so convinced I was going to Germany, I signed up for an accelerated German course that crammed two semesters of German into one and studied for a year and a half to prepare for the program. There were several German students living at I-House and I used every opportunity to practice speaking German. I took more German courses and by my senior year, I had earned just enough language credits to apply for the exchange program. My German skills were still rough and two of my professors were not entirely convinced I was ready for a year abroad. My persistence and confidence finally won them over and I was eventually selected to attend. Quite unexpectedly, however, the program was cancelled shortly before I was to leave. I was so convinced I was going, I couldn't accept this outcome. I refused to believe this would stop me.

More determined than ever, I found another way to get to Europe. I graduated a semester early, returned to Houston and spent the spring of 1979 playing in a touring orchestra with a regional opera theater. I also auditioned and received a scholarship to attend a summer music program in Graz, Austria. The program covered my living expenses for six weeks. All I needed was enough money to cover my flight and incidentals. The program was designed for young American singers and instrumentalists looking for professional opportunities in Europe. I decided this would be my vehicle to accomplish my goal, not as an exchange student, but as a professional musician.

By the end of the program, money was starting to run out. I needed a way to come up with enough cash to carry me over until I could find a job. My desire to live in Germany was so strong, the emotion so intense, it consumed my thoughts and drove me to take drastic action. In a flash, I made a bold decision to exchange the return portion of my flight ticket for $350 cash. I refused to think about the consequences of not having a way back home. I knew I would find a way to make this work. To paraphrase Napoleon Hill, I burned a bridge and left myself no possible way for retreat. I had to win or perish!

The desire to stay in Europe had become so overpowering, it drove me to this action and my mind was in perfect alignment with the goal. I shut out all other thoughts of doubt and fear and was buoyed by a strong sense of conviction that this was the right thing to do at the right time. Whenever negative thoughts surfaced, I would drown out their voices by shouting loudly in my head, "Go away! You're wrong! I'm going to prove to everyone that I can do this! Take that, all you naysayers who doubt me or think I can't!" That stubbornness and burning desire to "show them!" allowed the alignment to take place.

I left Austria and headed for Munich. In the center of town was a large public square. While there, I spotted a young man in the distance sitting by some steps, playing the guitar and harmonica. He was surrounded by a crowd of young people, mostly college students in jeans and smoking hand-rolled cigarettes. I could hear him singing the refrain of a popular song at the time, "the answer, my friend, is blowing in the wind. . . ." I walked up to the crowd to get a closer look. Young girls were singing along and clapping their hands together with the music. It was quite a festive atmosphere. Everyone appeared to be having a great time, including myself. At twenty-one, I looked just like every other young, bohemian student and fit right in. I glanced down at his open guitar case. There were only a few coins in it and nobody was tossing any money. I felt bad for him. He was definitely a crowd pleaser, but this crowd had no money. And suddenly, inspiration struck me like a lightning bolt and I rushed back to my hotel. I had a plan!

I was traveling with one suitcase and a violin. In the suitcase were jeans, t-shirts, one dress shirt, and . . . a tuxedo! I quickly showered and put on my tux, complete with bow tie and cummerbund, grabbed my violin, and went back to the square. The guitarist and his crowd were still there, so I went to the other side of the square as far away from them as I could get. The talents I learned as a strolling gypsy violinist were about to pay dividends. Dressed in formal attire, I played Strauss waltzes, Brahms Hungarian dances, Mozart, and Beethoven. I played beloved melodies and tunes from the 50s and from popular German operettas.

The crowd across the way laughed at me. They didn't take me seriously. "What a geek!" they must have thought. That did not stop me. I continued playing my heart out and an amazing thing started to happen. Middle-aged German women walking past me would stop and listen for a bit and then throw coins in my violin case. Lots of coins. Older people would stop and hear me play "The Blue Danube" and smile. Soon, the coins were outnumbered by bills and I had to periodically clean out my case to hide all the money I was collecting. Little old ladies swooned, "*Ach, wie süß!*" and praised me for "keeping the culture alive." It was like taking candy from a baby. I couldn't believe how this was happening! I played in the square for a day and a half and collected the German equivalent of $300.

I stopped when it became evident to me I had the means to generate money in a pinch. This was proof that the universe was telling me to proceed with my plans. More convinced than ever my dream was about to come true, I pushed on. And, within two weeks and with only one audition, I landed a concertmaster position with a small opera theater orchestra in Giessen, a small town just north of Frankfurt. I moved there immediately and performed in the orchestra for five seasons. And in that time, I not only learned to speak German fluently, I met my wife, got married, and traveled and performed extensively across the continent.

V. WHEN ACTION WAS KING

After five years of living my dream, I somehow outgrew it. It lost its allure and I no longer felt the passion I once had for living in Europe. The German *Wunderwirtschaft* economy had slowed down and political tensions began to heat up. My wife and I wanted to return to the States and start a family. It was time to move on. We settled in Houston, where I still had family. The economy in Houston in the mid 80s was even worse than what we left behind in Germany. All of the arts organizations in the city suffered large cut backs in funding just to stay afloat. For two years, I freelanced around town. The job opportunities were drying up and I was becoming increasingly frustrated with performing. Playing the violin no longer energized me. On the contrary, it sapped my energy. It brought me no pleasure. I started to dread going to the rehearsals and concerts. Our financial situation at home was very tight. We barely eked out enough money for a down payment on a small house. Soon after we moved in, our first child was born. Dreams of a concert career were replaced with fear, anxiety, and mounting stress. I took every job I could find. But I knew this situation was untenable.

I gravitated more toward my left brain and moved away from the heart. Passion wasn't going to pay the bills. I needed to "think" my way out of this funk. Alarm bells were going off all around me as my apprehension continued to grow. I did everything I could to bury those feelings deep inside me. I took comfort in the refuge of rational thinking, detached from emotion. It was time for me to grow up and behave like an adult. I found reassurance in logic and structure. I looked for rules to provide meaning and guidance and learned to trust them over intuition.

It was during this period in my life when I first read *Think and Grow Rich*. Although I initially found the section on desire quite familiar (having applied it intuitively in achieving my goal of living in Europe), it was Hill's "Thirty-One Causes of Failure" which resonated with me like the Ten Commandments. Here was a playbook of what not to do to avoid failure. By following these rules, I could reinvent myself, trade in my financially risky musical profession for a more practical and secure corporate career, and focus on building wealth.

And so, in another bold decision and with complete support from my wife, I signed up for classes at a vocational school to learn computer programming. It would take me six months of being a full time student again and, during that time, we would have to manage on my wife's income as an executive secretary. I knew it would be difficult for me to continue freelancing while I was in school, so I resigned from all the groups I had been performing with and notified the agencies. My decision to get out of music provoked unexpected and seriously negative reactions from many of my colleagues. Some felt I was betraying my art. Others accused me of selling out to corporate greed. A few even took my actions very personally which ended some longtime friendships. This was another "burning bridge" moment and there was no turning back. Six months went by very quickly and I proved to be a fast learner. Compared to German, computer languages were not difficult for me. I delighted in the mental constructs of software logic. By the time I finished school, I had developed an action plan with a roadmap on how I was going to increase my earning potential. I was about to turn thirty and had no time to lose! I reviewed and tweaked the plan daily. It became my obsession. The plan comprised a series of steps to quickly acquire a broad-based level of experience in various technology environments within the first five years. Rapid job movement and employer changes would allow for aggressive salary increases. The most challenging part of the plan was creating "the elevator speech" to land the first job.

After all, who would want to hire a concert violinist to write computer software?

It was January of 1987 and the economy in Houston was slowly rebounding. Many oil patch workers, geologists, and engineers had lost their jobs and retrained as computer programmers.

Computer science was a promising field, but the competition to find work was fierce. I knew I had to find a job quickly. I was ready to launch my action plan. The school offered some meager outplacement which didn't yield anything for me. Search firms were offering their services for a fee, but I didn't want to pay someone to find me a job.

Inspiration struck again! I knew there had to be companies on shoestring budgets in need of computer programmers. They would be more likely to take a gamble on someone like me. I immediately thought of the government. Not known for paying top dollar, experienced talent wouldn't be fishing in those waters. I searched the telephone directory and made cold calls to various city and county offices. One call was to the director of the Data Processing department in a neighboring county. I nearly fell out of my chair when he told me they had an opening for an entry level programmer with at least one year of experience. I talked him into letting me come in for an interview. After all, I already had six months of experience writing programs at school! I was hired within a week. My starting annual salary was $22K.

I kept loyal to my action plan. After a year at the county, I took a programming analyst job with a privately owned auto distributor for eighteen months, and then took a two year analyst contract with a natural gas pipeline company. With each successive move, I inched up the career ladder and accumulated experience in a number of business applications and industries. I was also able to get back to music part time. By April, 1991, I was recruited by an outside firm and offered a position as a software development manager overseeing a team of programmers at a medical supplies distributor. In just a little over four years of starting a new career, I moved into IT management and was making $60K. In the decade to follow

I relied on my action plan to move into three other business careers, each time doubling my income.

VI. TURNING POINT

Having more income at our disposal allowed us to acquire things, move into a bigger house, and enjoy frequent European vacations. Somehow, the more money I earned, the more trapped I felt. I was secure in a job I found increasingly unsatisfying and my world reflected a sterile, lifeless, bland existence.

In 2001, I moved into a new role as a Quality and Process Improvement director at a healthcare insurance company, which required 50–80% travel. In spite of the grueling schedule, I still freelanced here and there when time permitted. The pressure took its toll on me, physically. I developed a repetitive stress injury in my left hand and had to wear an arm brace for over a month followed by six weeks of physical therapy. I couldn't play the violin during that time. When I was able to start up again after therapy, I had to take baby steps. My strength and dexterity were far from a hundred percent. My spirit was crushed at how difficult it was for me to play the simplest things. I stopped playing the violin altogether, said good-bye to my life as a violinist, and threw myself into my work. A growing sense of unease was welling up within me, and the more I tried to quash it, the more it would surface.

During this time, I lived out of a suitcase, gained weight, ate too much fast food, smoked, and stopped exercising. It was chest pain and a trip to the emergency room in 2005 that served as my wakeup call. My health was suffering. My high paying job was unfulfilling and stressful. My life style was killing me. I felt disconnected emotionally and not aligned to my purpose. I was in trouble. How had my life strayed so far away from the halcyon days of a traveling street musician? What lessons did I need to learn to move past this?

Reluctant to change the formula I had been following for almost two decades, I once more called upon behavior and logic to guide me. I developed another action plan to get me back on track. I set new goals for myself. I engaged in new behaviors. I quit smoking. I joined a medically supervised weight management program at a hospital and lost weight. I went back to the gym and started exercising again. I began reading personal development and spirituality books, including those of John Randolph Price. I started meditating and kept a journal. I attended spiritual retreats. I cleared emotional blocks through the healing power of essential oils, prayer and music. I wanted to understand the unconscious beliefs programmed deep inside me. I was looking for answers to spiritual questions and wanted to know what my purpose was.

I reread *Think and Grow Rich*. I focused this time on the power of belief. Hill wrote, "your subconscious mind recognizes and acts only upon thoughts that have been well mixed with emotion or feeling. . . . You will get no appreciable results until you learn to reach your subconscious mind with thoughts, or spoken words that have been well emotionalized with belief." I was ready to let go of old beliefs and create new ones. I applied autosuggestion to change the beliefs that were no longer resourceful to me.

And amidst all the flurry of these endeavors, a new level of understanding revealed itself to me. I had to acknowledge that what I had experienced was exactly what I set in motion. I had been rewarded with what I wanted in life—financial security. In my quest for success, I turned a blind eye to happiness, health, and well being. The secret had, in fact, delivered its end of the bargain. It was in this moment of clarity I realized I could no longer suppress my passion for life and my emotions. I needed to honor them, along with the intellect, and my penchant for action, in a balanced, harmonious way.

VII. WHEN THOUGHT REIGNED

Hill describes faith as emotionalized thought. "Thoughts that are mixed with any of the feelings of emotions constitute a "magnetic" force, which attracts similar or related thoughts." It took me years of analysis to recognize that along with the conscious desire to be rich, coursing through my body was a set of emotionally charged unconscious beliefs that attracted people and situations to me. Some of these beliefs were useful and reassuring: "I will always be taken care of financially. I will never be without money." And that has always been the case. It still works for me even today. Other beliefs, however, have clearly worked against me: "I don't deserve lavish abundance, only meager subsistence. I will have only enough money to meet my modest needs and avoid poverty." The conscious mental images supporting my desire for accumulating great wealth were no match for these core beliefs. My thoughts and emotions were conflicted. Although I fantasized often of having unlimited wealth, without the intense, emotional commitment to sustain the belief with true conviction, there was little chance the goal would materialize. And that's exactly what happened. The more money I manifested in my life, the more it flowed out. My earning power increased multiple-fold, but my net worth remained constant.

My core beliefs weren't just about money. They applied in the same way to my health, wellbeing and happiness. I was short-changing myself emotionally, physically, and financially. These beliefs affected not only me, but my family, friends, and coworkers. It was time for another moment of inspiration, of bold action, and burning bridges. The inspiration came quietly to me during one of my morning meditations. "Let it all go," I heard the voice inside me say. "Let go of the need to control. Allow your intuition to guide you. Give your mind a rest. John, it's easier than you think." And so, I reluctantly did. I began a sixty day "Non-Human" program outlined in John Randolph Price's book, *A Spiritual Philosophy for the New World.* The program was designed to allow one to "rise above the ego" and consisted of daily meditation, journaling, and "letting go." Instead of asking for things or searching for solutions to problems, the meditations focused entirely on contemplating my Higher Self. The burning bridge for me this time was the most challenging one to date. It meant giving up my mental need for structure and answers. I had to let go of control and turn the wheel over to intuition to do the driving. And, for this to work, I had to do so *willingly.*

At first I focused on loving and appreciating everything and everyone around me, including myself. This meant smiling at people, taking the time to listen to them and doing whatever I could to ease their burden. At airports, I made a point of being cheerful to gate agents and flight attendants. I assisted other passengers with their belongings. I even offered my free first class upgrade to a woman who clearly looked like she needed a break. Just seeing her face light up when I asked her to swap boarding passes was worth the deed. At work, I focused on doing what needed to get done to please my boss. When I felt stressed, I took extra time to greet coworkers and staff and looked for ways to convey gratitude and appreciation to each of them. I said "thank you" as often as I could without sounding ridiculous. I started to like myself a lot more and, over time, my days on the road were turning out to become much more pleasant and fun. My step was lighter and my stress level went down. I got my groove back and looked forward to going to work each day. And the people around me started to smile more and laugh. Meetings required less effort. I was enjoying my work. Projects ran smoother. Issues resolved themselves with less work and more ease. Relationships became more harmonious. Dread and anxiety vanished.

As my world changed around me, I knew this was evidence that something good was happening to me. My core beliefs were starting to shift. What I was attracting into my life reflected that shift. I had reconnected with my emotions and they were aligned to my nascent core beliefs. My understanding and emotional connection to abundance expanded to include other areas of my life. I could see and feel a common thread connecting material wealth, loving relationships, health, wellbeing, and definite purpose. Through their interconnection, each aspect was benefiting from the energetic flow.

Soon, job opportunities in Houston started to present themselves. One, in particular, showed up in my email inbox from a career search website. It was the ultimate dream job and mother lode of all I could imagine! An opportunity to lead a team and build an organization for a recognized, award winning, national leader in healthcare; considered one of the best places to work for in the Houston metropolitan area; excellent pay; a talented, energetic team; an awesome boss looking for someone with my skills; an office location only ten minutes away from home; and, best of all, no travel! Finally, my evenings and weekends could be spent at home with my family and pursuing other interests instead of checking into and out of hotels and boarding gates. Yes, this was my dream job. I just needed to find a way to have them hire me!

The hiring process took about two months. It started with several rounds of intense interviews with the HR recruiter, the hiring manager, the staff, and my peers. Each time I showed up for another round of interviews, the field narrowed. And I became more and more excited about the possibility of getting an offer. And throughout this time I kept my daily regimen of meditation and journaling and sending out positive love vibes. The interviews were going well. I was poised and felt confident. I smiled a lot and showed much grace under fire. I knew I had it in the bag!

By the end of the process I was one of only two candidates left. There was one final interview with the senior executive. As I waited outside her office at the appointed time, I could feel deep inside me, a tiny sprout from that old belief of unworthiness starting to rise up and interlace itself in my new beliefs. I could feel it take hold, feeding off the fear welling within me. I started to doubt myself. I panicked. Why this? Why now? I took several deep breaths and tried unsuccessfully to redirect my thoughts. By the time I was escorted to the office and introduced to the executive, the easy feeling of confidence and poise had all but left me. As I answered questions and attempted to carry on a composed discussion, a loud voice within me was shouting, "What are you doing? You do not belong here. You don't deserve this kind of happiness. Who are you kidding? You're blowing it! She sees right through you." I left the interview completely convinced I had derailed myself. Dejected and crestfallen, I knew I was not going to get this job.

And I was right. The other guy got the offer and accepted. In the rejection letter, the hiring manager said it was extremely close. My credentials were on par with the other candidate, but he had a certain something they were looking for which gave him the edge. I was surprised in how I reacted to the news.

My old self would have gotten angry, lashed out, and wallow in pity, self loathing, and guilt. My new self looked at this as a learning experience. I took full responsibility for the outcome and resisted the urge to cast blame on myself or anyone else. I knew I had more work to do in deprogramming my old beliefs. "When I'm ready, I will attract another opportunity into my life." That is what I chose to believe as part of my new reality.

Throughout this time period, I continued to commute back and forth between Houston and Connecticut. As my mood and outlook improved, I began to miss the violin more and more. Seven years had already gone by since my decision to stop playing. Although I missed performing, I told myself those days were behind me. Occasionally, I would take the violin out of the case and play at home. My wife and daughters were delighted when I would do this and constantly encouraged me to play again. But, I chose not to listen. It was too late, I thought. No use.

Four months went by since the job interview and I received another email in my inbox about a job opening. It was for the *same* position at the *same* company! What was going on? How could that be? I deliberated for a moment. Should I apply again? They didn't want me before, why would they want me now? And then I said to myself, "Hold on! I WANT this! And this time I'm READY!" I sent an email directly to the hiring manager asking her to consider having me post for the position again. I got a response that same day saying how pleased she was to hear from me and offered to move me all the way to the final round so that I wouldn't have to go through the interview process all over again. Suddenly, I felt the excitement returning. I had been given a second chance. This time was going to be different. I was in a much better place, emotionally, than only four months before.

Timing was on my side. I was just preparing to leave for a four day spiritual development workshop in Boerne, Texas. I set my intention to get to the bottom of my belief issues once and for all.

I knew if I could erase the lingering sense of unworthiness from my consciousness, those thoughts would not come back to sabotage me. The theme of the workshop was "A New Dawn Awakening." How apropos as I reflected what was about to happen in my life.

It was at the workshop that I had a breakthrough releasing a lot of old, unconscious emotional baggage. The release was profound and I recognized my major definite purpose was to heal others through the use of my musical talents and other gifts I had learned. I stood up in front of the group in one of the sessions and declared my intention to start playing the violin again. I further committed to bringing the violin with me to the next gathering six months later to perform for them. It was an exhilarating feeling. I felt whole again. And my consciousness changed. The feelings of unworthiness subsided. They no longer made sense in my new understanding of myself. Replacing them were new thoughts reflecting a much different self image. "I have everything now, for I have been given the Kingdom. There is nothing missing in my life, and I let the fullness of the Kingdom come forth now into perfect expression."

Literally, over night, my world changed yet again. The following morning I received a phone call from a music contractor I hadn't heard from in years. "John, I know you stopped playing a while ago, but I'm in a bind and could really use your help. I have three Christmas concerts coming up in less than a month and I need a strong concertmaster to lead the orchestra. I'll offer you double scale rates if you're willing to do this." My jaw dropped. Before I could think this through, I immediately accepted all three jobs and thanked him for reaching out to me. I wasn't sure yet how I would manage getting the time off from work, but I knew I had to do this. I would also need the next few weeks to get back into musical shape and buy a new tux.

The day after the phone call, I received a follow up email from the hiring manager with a date for the final interview. During the interview I wanted to know what happened to the guy they hired just a few months before. It wasn't the right fit after all. He didn't last long and left the company to take another position elsewhere. And, when I inquired about the feedback from the senior executive I met with the first go around, it turned out she was very impressed with me. (Clearly the voices in my head during that meeting did quite a number on me!). My reality had changed and a week later I was offered and had accepted the position. By December 2008, I started a new job (which I love even more today), traded my travel and airline platinum status for evenings and weekends at home, and returned to active performing. As if one giant tidal wave of abundance had suddenly flooded my world, I was awash in a lavish bounty of professional, personal, musical, and emotional riches. Hill's secret performed again for me, just as faithfully as in the past. My thoughts, emotions, and actions were aligned once more, this time in harmony with definite purpose. The integration was complete.

CONCLUSION

Reflecting on my life, I have been blessed with many wonderful experiences and demonstrations of the secret formula. Whether the goal was to live abroad, generate income, or create happiness and joy, the principles described in *Think and*

Grow Rich are timeless and universal. And they continue to render service as I create my reality.

Hill summed it up best when he said, "these are the steps that are essential for success in all walks of life . . . [which] lead to freedom and independence of thought . . . to riches in small or great quantities . . . that guarantee favorable 'breaks' . . . [that] convert dreams into physical realities . . . [and] mastery of fear, discouragement, and indifference . . . [and, for the] privilege of writing one's own ticket, and of making life yield whatever price is asked." At this moment in my life, I can honestly say I have achieved each of these results. And, it's a very good feeling.

About John Cramer

John Cramer directs the Organization Effectiveness program at a large regional healthcare system located in Houston, Texas. John is an innovator, a certified Six Sigma Master Black Belt, and a professional violinist. You can reach him at jcramer3@comcast.net.

18

Universal Truths Echoed by Napoleon Hill

by Rev. Dr. Sam Boys
DONALDSON, INDIANA

"The world inside your head is bigger
than the world outside your head."
–SOCRATES

There are two phrases that have been among the important guiding principles in my life the past several years. One, which on the surface appears to be a new-age cliché (but is in fact very *old*-age wisdom) is, "Where the mind goes—energy flows." And the second phrase is one that my Dad taught me many years ago: simply stated, "Plan your work—then work your plan." These two truths are at the same time both very simple and very difficult. They have been told and re-told for many generations and they show up throughout the ages in literature, mythology, science, philosophy, and even sacred texts. These truths are also most clearly articulated in profound ways in the works of Napoleon Hill. Basic principles like these are emphasized in *Think and Grow Rich* by outlining steps toward success and prosperity like setting a definite purpose, and channeling one's burning desire through applied faith and controlled attention.

In this chapter, I would like to draw a connection between the truths found in *Think and Grow Rich*, and also in the New Testament—specifically the narrative of Jesus and Peter walking on the water, found in Matthew 14: 22–33. The following is a paraphrase of this ancient story. I should like to call it:

Peter Walks on the Water . . . Almost
or
Three Feet from Salvation

As our story opens, Jesus' disciples are out on a boat in the middle of the sea. Jesus is not with them because he has stayed behind on shore to minister to the crowds of people gathered there. As evening approaches, it begins to grow dark, and a storm is brewing. The wind begins to pick-up and causes huge waves to churn and slosh into the boat so that the boat is tossed to and fro. This continues all night. The disciples battle the storm, desperately trying to stay afloat.

And just before dawn they look out over the water and see a ghost-like figure approaching. They are terrified. As the figure continues closer to them, they hear a voice, "Don't be afraid. It's me!" Then they recognize that it is Jesus. Peter gets so excited that he immediately steps out of the boat, onto the water, and starts walking—almost running on the water toward Jesus. Just when he is almost there he stops. He takes his eyes off his goal. He no longer looks at Jesus, but becomes afraid. Looking around him he sees the wind and surging waves and he thinks, "Hey . . . what am I doing? I can't walk on the water." And it is at that precise moment that he sinks. Blub . . . blub . . . blub. Then Jesus reaches down and grabs his hand and pulls him back up, so that they are now both standing on the water once again. And Jesus says to Peter, "Why were you afraid? Don't you have any faith?" Then they get into the boat. The wind dies down. The sun comes out. And there they all sit—in total amazement.

This is an extraordinary story, yet it reveals a scene all too common in our human experience. It tells us many things. First it begins in darkness and chaos. Storms are powerful metaphors for chaos and fear, and darkness for unknowing and struggle akin to what St. John of the Cross has called the dark night of the soul. This state of being is common in our everyday world, for many people in our world live fear. Fear of change. Fear of the unknown. Fear of failure. Fear of new things. We're afraid of dying. We're afraid of living. We have been conditioned to stay in our own settled paradigms never fully stepping out into new ventures, because we don't believe we can. We have been so conditioned by our daily lives that we actually buy the idea that we have no control—that the outside world is somehow more real than the internal world. We have been socialized to believe that all the events and circumstances around us already determine what happens to us. Dr. Hill is saying just the opposite. One of the brilliant truths revealed by his writings is that: it's what is *within* us that creates what's outside of us. As we think—so we are. Or, as Napoleon Hill says, "Whatever your mind can conceive and believe, your mind can achieve."

This shows up in the story of Jesus and Peter. First of all, in their doubt and fear, the disciples couldn't even see beyond their own worldview. They didn't even recognize that it was Jesus at first. Then Peter broke free of this paradigm—just for a moment—when, in his zeal, he was able to see his definite purpose. Like Andrew Carnegie in Hill's book, his goal was more than a wish—it was a burning desire—an opportunity to be acted upon with courage and verve. So Peter, at first, is able to act upon his desire with a deep and genuine faith, and he does so immediately, without procrastination.

And Peter kept his attention on his goal. Once he fixed his attention on his major purpose, he focused his controlled attention on that goal. Then acted. (Here echoes the two truths mentioned at the beginning of this chapter: "Where the mind goes—energy flows." and "Plan your work—then work your plan.") As Dr. Hill reminds us, concentration and focus on a single goal has been the hallmark of success for countless people and organizations. When our dominating thoughts are fixed on our purpose—then anything is possible. Even walking on water. How many of us can walk on water? If we can't could it be that we have been conditioned to believe that it is not possible? But Peter let all that go for a brief moment, and was able to manifest a new reality.

Here it is again. The power of our intention. We need to work at training our subconscious mind—planting that inception of thought. Dr. Hill has explained it this way: because our subconscious minds are imprinted with so many other 'programs' and thoughts, once our minds are impressed with the object of our definite purpose, it will swing into action on its own—rendering up ideas, plans, and hunches whose clarity and applicability will surprise us. Peter literally lost his mind for a moment. He was so intent on his goal, that those old 'programs' that tell him it's impossible to walk on water were suddenly silenced.

It all begins with a thought. Thoughts trigger emotions, and emotions produce a physical response in our body which then leads to action. So our thoughts manifest into tangible form. This is the basic truth of the universe. The un-manifest takes material form. How is it that something as immaterial as a thought can produce something tangible like riches or prosperity? It involves many things. Our ability to choose is paramount. It's what sets us apart as human beings. We have the capacity for free choice and free inquiry. We are the makers of our own reality. We are that consciousness that drives the vehicle. We choose from unending waves of possibility to fix our experience.

Next is applied faith. Jesus makes it very clear that doing something extraordinary and unimaginable (like walking on water) requires deep faith. A firm conviction that it *is* possible. Napoleon Hill's Principles remind us that, "Faith is our awareness of, belief in, and harmonizing with the universal powers. We should not simply have faith; we must use it." Hill reminds us that it is impossible to have active, applied faith without a definite belief in a supreme power—an Infinite Intelligence. Peter had this belief, but he also had moments where, like many of us, our doubts and fears overtake us. Overcoming fear, conquering our disbelief, and replacing them with hope (not 'wishful thinking'—but a genuine core belief) is the way to use our applied faith to reach our goal.

Like the gold miners in *Think and Grow Rich* (who, in their exhaustion and doubt stopped digging when, unbeknownst to them they were only three feet from striking it rich), Peter was so close to reaching his goal when doubt and fear overcame him. He took his eyes off of Jesus and looked around at the waves and began to realize that he was standing on the water out in the middle of the sea. He may have only been three feet from Jesus! It was right then and there that he sank. Jesus' response to this was, "Why were you afraid? Don't you have any faith?" Doubt and fear are indeed obstacles to overcome if we are to achieve our goal. We must work through rather than avoid these obstacles.

In our modern age, with such a fast-paced lifestyle, there are other obstacles to overcome. The greatest of which is our tendency toward distraction. This is even more of a challenge today than it was in Napoleon Hill's time. It is clear from our story that, not only did Peter succumb to doubt and fear, but at the root of his demise was his distracted attention.

Distraction—literally getting off-track. This happens all too often in our modern technological world. How many of us have ever experienced talking with someone and find ourselves smiling and nodding, and making eye contact with the person who is speaking, yet our minds are somewhere else? Outwardly we may appear to be listening, but our attention is divided. We're there—but not really there. Suddenly we realize we haven't heard a word the other person was saying. We have missed the moment. We have missed the connection with that other human being who is right in front of us.

Another scenario: Imagine meeting someone in a crowded sports bar (perhaps a client, a friend, a loved one) and you are trying to hold a conversation with them. And the whole time, the other person is constantly glancing at one or two or five of the several television screens behind and over your shoulder, they check their cell phone for text messages, and are constantly diverting their gaze to the people who keep walking by.

We are living in a split-screen world. We can no longer watch a show on television anymore without continuous pop-ups and crawls and other visuals that pull our attention away from the show we are watching. And the show we were watching is also chopped-up into smaller and smaller segments between commercials. The commercials come so often and last so long that it is almost impossible to maintain a sense of continuity with the show. Even the commercials themselves become shorter and shorter—squeezing in more commercials per break.

These are just a few examples of what is now considered to be the norm. It is common for such scenarios to occur on a daily basis. The way we live today seems to be actually changing the way we think, and the way we process information. We don't seem to go very deep in any one subject for very long. In fact, I, myself, have been conditioned by our modern lifestyle and find that I have to really make an effort to sit and read for a long period of time. It is becoming increasingly more difficult to maintain deep, sustained focused attention—in relationships, in our jobs, in our driving, and in our everyday life. At any given moment, ask yourself: "How many places am I right now, besides right here? Where is my attention right now? Is my mind truly on my goal, or am I distracted by something else?" (Where the mind goes—energy flows).

I have noticed this in my own experience in teaching. Many students today cannot even endure a one-hour class without checking their cell phones. As the classroom discussion or lecture ensues, nearly every time, a cell phone rings or someone feels the need to check their incoming messages. So the question I ask is: "Is your text message more important than what is going on in class right now? If so, why are you even in class? And what does that tell your professor about the importance you place on what goes on in the classroom?"

Rarely do students sit and ponder the mysteries of the universe anymore. In my college days, I remember spending hours sitting under a tree thinking . . . watching . . . reflecting . . . just being alone with my thoughts. Do students today ever spend time sitting alone with themselves in silence . . . deep in thought? Do *any* of us allow ourselves to simply be still? It is my experience that we do not. Or cannot. We have to be constantly engaged in some activity. Some distraction.

People are so dazed that they have almost no time to reflect on the world around them. "Nearly a third of workers feel they often do not have time to reflect on or process the work they do. More than half typically juggle too many tasks simultaneously. One yearlong study found that workers not only switch tasks every three minutes during their workday but that nearly half the time they interrupt themselves."

Sociologist Maggie Jackson, in her book *Distraction*, asks, "Is all this progress? We have reason to worry. Kids are the inveterate multitaskers, the technologically fluent new breed that is better suited for the lightning-paced, many-threaded digital world, right? After all, they are bathed in an average of nearly six hours a day of nonprint media content, and a quarter of that time they are using more than one screen, dial, or channel. Nearly a third of fourteen- to twenty-one-year-olds juggle five to eight media while doing homework."

Yet, for all their high-tech fluency, these same kids show a remarkably low percentage in critical reasoning skills, patience, and problem-solving skills related to analytical reasoning. Jackson concludes that "we can't be a nation of reflective, analytic problem solvers while cultivating a culture of distraction. I am not alone in wondering how often our children will experience the hard-fought pleasures of plunging deeply into a thought, a conversation, a state of being. Will focusing become a lost art, quaintly exhibited alongside blacksmithing at the historic village? ('Look, honey, that man in the twentieth-century costume is doing just one thing!')." It seems we are all getting more adept at multi-tasking, and at the same time, less able to focus solely on one task fully, deeply, and thoroughly.

SO . . . what's the solution? How can we live in this high-tech, multi-tasking, split-screen world of distraction and still remain clear and focused and calm? When our attention is so scattered and divided it is like shining a beam of light that gets diffused in so many directions. And when the light gets diffused, it becomes dimmer. If our beam of light could shine on just one thing—how bright our light would be! But, since there are so many demands on our attention, our light beam gets scattered. How can we focus that light? How can we make that light stronger?

Think of the metaphor of a lighthouse. Its beam of light shines brightly—all around. But it doesn't scatter its light. It is a full beam of light that moves from one thing to the next—fully focused on one thing at a time. As the beam moves, it shines its full strength on each object, and then moves on to the next. If we could be more like a lighthouse, we could focus 100% on one thing at a time. Singular focus is much more powerful than multiple foci. And when we bring this definiteness of purpose into our lives, our relationships grow stronger, our careers flourish, and our mind becomes clearer. And clarity of mind is a key ingredient to success and well-being.

Back to Jesus and his disciples. He continually reminds us, in teachings like the Sermon on the Mount in Matthew's Gospel, that we are the Light of the World, and to let our Light shine! To stay focused on our goal (for no one can serve two masters) and apply our faith with a burning desire, and then to put that faith into action by moving decisively and intentionally toward that goal (plan your work—work your plan). Otherwise, if we allow the wind and waves of doubt & fear to overtake us—if we become distracted and take our eyes off the prize—then we will sink.

Napoleon Hill reminds us all that faith exists only so long as it is put into action. And the key to a living faith is to, first and foremost, have a positive mental attitude. Once we do, then we can adopt our definite major purpose, affirm the object of our desire through prayer—day and night—and run with perseverance the race that is set before us.

I would like to conclude by sharing a thought from Napoleon Hill's *Keys to Success*:

"Close the door of fear behind you, and you will quickly see the door of faith open before you. Increasing and applying your faith is a process that takes time and dedication. You will never be finished with this task because the power you have at your disposal is infinite. So are the rewards."

About Rev. Dr. Sam Boys

Rev. Dr. Sam Boys is Associate Professor of Philosophy and Religion at Ancilla College in Donaldson, Indiana. He has recently released a book and audio CD on the healing power of Breath and Sound. You can reach him directly by e-mail at didjeridude@rocketmail.com

19

We Reap What We Sow

by Christina Chia
KUALA LUMPUR, MALAYSIA

It is said that the secret in *Think and Grow Rich* is no secret. You already know it and you have it. What then is this secret that will jump out of each page to meet you?

To me the answer is found in the very first chapter: "thoughts are things." The rest of the 13 principles are the how-to, showing you the steps to stimulate quality thoughts to help you achieve your heart's desires. If you are able to tap deeper within yourself, you can learn to step up the vibration of your thoughts to sharpen your intuition or your sixth sense. The last chapter reveals the six ghosts of fear and a person's susceptibility to negative influences which you must be aware of and protect yourself against.

Can we really think and grow rich? Yes we can. All of us can think and grow rich. It is a fact that everything begins with a seed of thought. Thought is the only thing over which we have complete control. No one can do the thinking for us. If it's going to be, it's up to us. We have a conscious mind which gives us the power to choose our thoughts. Once the seed of a thought is planted in the subconscious mind, the subconscious will strive to give us what we have planted. The function of the subconscious mind is to give you what you want. Literally we reap what we sow. If you plant the seed of thoughts of riches in your "mind garden," you can grow rich.

Dr. Hill used his subconscious to find the title, *Think and Grow Rich*. His publisher thought the title used on the manuscript, *Thirteen Steps to Riches*, lacked the "ring" of a successful book. Dr. Hill tried over 500 titles and none suited him, and as time came to go to press, the publisher set an ultimatum: give him the title by the next day or he'd go with the title he liked, *Use Your Noodle and Get Your Boodle*. Faced with such a horrible consequence, Hill used his knowledge of autosuggestion to get his subconscious in high gear—talking himself into such a state of emotion the neighbors thought he was quarreling with his wife. By the middle of the night, Hill's subconscious had hit upon the now-famous, short and sweet, *Think and Grow Rich*.

My advice to you is to be mindful of your thoughts. Through the use of the 13 steps in *Think and Grow Rich*, your mind may be stimulated to come up with creative thoughts, with ideas. It's been said that you are never short of money, only ideas. Indeed ideas can be translated into money. Ideas that come to you may be like flickering sparks: you have to fan them until they erupt into flame and become your burning desire.

Ralph Waldo Emerson said "One single idea may have greater weight than the labor of all the people, animals and engines for a century." So remember to give life to your idea. Plant your ideas in your mind garden for eternity. May you think and grow rich.

About Christina Chia

Christina Chia is the Founder of Napoleon Hill Associates (NHA) and has organized Napoleon Hill International Conventions in 2007 and 2010. She is a practicing corporate attorney by profession and is the Founding Partner of CHRISTINA CHIA LAW CHAMBERS, a law firm based in Kuala Lumpur, Malaysia. Recently she has authored MIND GARDEN, a book dealing with motivational, self-help practices. She can be reached through NHA's website at www.nha2u.com.

If the thing you wish to do is right, and you believe in it, go ahead and do it! Put your dream across, and never mind what "they" say if you meet with temporary defeat, for "they," perhaps, do not know that every failure brings with it the seed of an equivalent success.

—NAPOLEON HILL

20

Change the Philosophy into a Habit

by Michael Telapary
BURGH-HAAMSTEDE, NETHERLANDS

In the first chapter of *Think and Grow Rich*, Napoleon Hill tells the story about Edwin C. Barnes. This man had a dream and turned it into a burning desire. Physically he had nothing to start with, but mentally he was fully prepared: he had a definite purpose of becoming the business associate of the great Thomas Edison. His burning desire was so powerful that it overruled all possible problems, adversities or temporary defeats.

That, in a nutshell, is the secret of the book. If you can see it, dream it, you can make it come true. Let me tell you how I've applied the secret.

In 1908 Napoleon Hill crossed paths with Andrew Carnegie and within a few days, work commenced on the project that would become *Think and Grow Rich*. Exactly 100 years later, in August 2008, my road crossed with Judith Williamson's at the World Learning Center through a simple email. I've read *Think and Grow Rich* several times but I still remember how the first time I started to read the book, I couldn't stop. The information in the book gave me goose-bumps. For me it was a mixture of things that are new to me and things that I have known all the time. It made me so curious that I kept on reading the book over and over again. I looked at my life and discovered that many of the principles written in the book I had already applied in the past to a certain extent.

I wanted to know more about Napoleon Hill and about his philosophy, so I composed an email to Judith with a story about how I used Hill's technique of tuning into another person's subconscious mind, to get specialized information that helped me to create a few incredible photorealistic airbrush paintings.

That one click on the email "Send" button would change my whole perception of the world.

After reading my story and viewing the paintings on my website, Judith wrote back with a proposition: could I create 17 artworks that would represent the 17 principles of Napoleon Hill? (In the first place I was surprised that she was talking about 17 principles, because I had only read *Think and Grow Rich* and it covers only 13 principles.)

It took me a couple of hours to think about it, and my burning desire to find out everything about the Napoleon Hill philosophy blocked me from rational thinking. Actually it was insane to say yes to a person I had never met, to create a series of 17 artworks in exchange of getting more information about the Napoleon Hill philosophy—in fact I worked on the project every day for 8 months, often more than 12 hours a day. Nevertheless I took action immediately and sent Judith an email with the answer, "Yes, I'm honored to create the 17 artworks." I was convinced this was an opportunity that would bring me closer than ever to my definite purpose.

The first artwork was also one of the most important principles to start with, "definiteness of purpose." Napoleon Hill talks repeatedly about a definite major purpose in life, and the force that is carried within a definite purpose. I had a definite major purpose, and that was to learn enough about the philosophy, to be able to apply it with success.

I have been airbrushing for more than 25 years, and in the last years of my airbrush period, I learned the technique of photorealistic airbrushing. The strange thing is that although I only created four paintings using that particular technique, the results were so astonishing that the viewers of my art were confused. One part of their brain told them it was a photograph, while another part refused to believe it, because some sections of the painting were impossible to capture with a camera.

When I said yes to Judith's request, I knew it was based on the photorealistic airbrush paintings she saw on my website. I also knew from the philosophy that you have to take action even if the first plan is not yet ready. So that same week I totally rebuilt my regular office into an airbrush studio—winter was coming and I didn't want to be out in my work shed studio, plus I didn't want to be separated from my wife Karin every day. It was lots of work building an air-supply system in the house which wouldn't make an annoying sound all day long.

I was fully prepared to start with my first artwork "Definiteness of Purpose." I had an idea in my mind and as usual I started making sketches, using computer graphic software like Photoshop. When my low-resolution composition was ready I emailed it to Judith so we could brainstorm about the idea. Judith really liked the whole thing and said it was ok. I told her I was glad she liked it, because now the real painting process could start, but Judith didn't understand my reaction; she said, "I thought this *was* the final artwork."

In that moment my subconscious mind started to work overtime to change the whole plan, and it made me say to Judith, "OK, no problem, if you want the artworks digitally, I can do that, I could use 3D software to make high resolution paintings, ready for high quality art-prints if necessary, and the advantage of digital artwork is, that we can make changes during the whole process." Now this is a good example of what your subconscious mind can do for you if you have a definite purpose: it hands over to you new ideas and plans to get closer to your goal, and where necessary it will change the plans. I had faith in my definite purpose, that I would finish those 17 artworks no matter what. But right after Judith gave approval to make them digitally, I realized that I had no real knowledge or experience about 3D software—and I had just rebuilt my whole office into an operational airbrush studio.

The solution came to me quickly: I had to buy new 3D software and follow all the necessary courses to work with it. I had enough determination to learn everything I needed to know about 3D software and applied it to create my final artwork of "Definiteness of Purpose" in high resolution, ready for print. That was almost 2 years ago, I haven't touched my airbrush since. Big successes don't come overnight; most of them take years of mental and physical preparation, waiting for the right opportunity. Although I had to start from the beginning with new tools, techniques and knowledge, I turned the adversity into its physical counterpart, success.

The Napoleon Hill art project was an amazing experience for me, transforming me both mentally and physically. Many works I did in the first months were totally redone later, because not only had my understanding and practice of the philosophy grown, but also my skills in digital artwork were much better. One of the first principles that I followed was writing my definite major purpose, which I read aloud two times a day until I could dream it. When I read my statement I read it with emotion, because I knew the thoughts behind the words had to be intensified to be picked up by the subconscious mind. I repeated that statement consistently for 8 months until the last day of the project. I did not share it with anyone but myself, but I will show you now so you can understand what can happen.

On April 30th 2009, I Michael Telapary will accomplish the assignment of 17 artworks that represent the 17 Napoleon Hill's principles of success.

In return I will invest all the necessary time to master digital art, and I will study the Napoleon Hill philosophy in depth to make sure that every specific artwork will radiate the motivational power that accompanies its principle.

I will make use of my mastermind alliance, which consists of Karin, Judith, and myself.

I believe that I will accomplish this assignment by April 30. My belief in this is so powerful that I can really touch the printed versions of the 17 artworks. They are hanging on the wall in my studio.

I will use all the plans, ideas and hunches that are necessary to achieve this goal, immediately at the time I receive them.

On April 30, 2009, at 11:45 pm, my last painting came off my wide-format printer.

Knowing the secret is not enough; the big challenge comes when you have to apply the principles successfully into your daily life. By using autosuggestion, reading the so-called hidden secret in the chapters over and over again, the subconscious mind will pick it up and change the philosophy into a habit.

About Michael Telapary

Michael Telapary is an artist and musician who has worked for more than 25 years as an entrepreneur in the retail business. As a certified instructor for the Napoleon Hill Foundation he has found many ways to invoke the 17 success principles in his creative projects—especially in his art and music. One of his major chief aims is to spread the Napoleon Hill philosophy throughout the world. Performing and conducting workshops are two powerful tools that he utilizes to reach groups of people. For more information about his projects, visit his website at www.tewanka.com.

21

Scotoma: Do You Have It?

by Fred Wikkeling
SAN JOSE, CALIFORNIA

As I'm preparing my thoughts for this chapter, one word pops into my mind: *scotoma*. Do you know what scotoma is? Almost everyone has it, some more than others—and worst of all, you don't even know if you have it.

The dictionary definition of scotoma is, "An area of diminished vision within the visual field." In other words, a blind spot. Although scotoma is a physical malady, I think it applies to all of us, because we suffer *mental* blind spots. Like the saying goes, "I can't see the forest because the trees are in the way."

You may have missed the secret in *Think and Grow Rich* in the same way. The most obvious secrets are the instructions for the self mastery of the material in the chapters. Napoleon Hill tells you what to do, and the secrets are right in front of your nose. It is my sincerest purpose and desire that you will see, feel, and hear the many secrets that Napoleon Hill so eloquently sprinkled on the pages of this classic book.

The secret is not one secret but many. If you are just looking for one secret, reread the book again with open eyes, searching each page for multiple clues, ideas, specific formulas and suggestions. The secrets are the supportive principles and formulas that transfer intangible thoughts, ideas, dreams and goals into tangible realities that are goods and services. Napoleon Hill instructs you with principles and formulas and then gives you documented stories as verification and exemplification.

Let me give a couple of hints that might help you. Remember that each chapter's title is a key secret. For instance, in chapter one's subtitle, "thought and desire turned into a fortune," we see an intangible thought turned into millions of tangible dollars, the fortune.

Also remember that throughout the book Dr. Hill uses italics to expose key secrets. Again from chapter one, "One of the chief characteristics of Barnes' desire was it was *definite*. He wanted to work *with* Edison not *for* him. . . . *But there was something in the expression of his face which conveyed the impression that he was determined to get what he had come after.*" Edison gives Barnes the opportunity to work with him "*because I saw he had made up his mind to stand by until he succeeded.*" Do you see how Hill is showing you the secrets?

Keeping these tips in mind, follow me through some of the topics I've found most important in my study of *Think and Grow Rich*.

The title of the first chapter, "Thoughts Are Things," is the first and foremost secret. Dr. Hill explains, "Truly, thoughts are things and powerful things at that, when they are mixed with a definiteness of purpose, persistence, and a burning desire for their translation into riches, or other material objects." Dr. Hill refers to riches in many different facets. Most people think only of financial riches. However riches can come in the mental, physical, and spiritual realms as well as the "great riches in lasting friendships, harmonious family relationships, sympathy and understanding between business associates, and inner harmony which brings peace of mind measurable only in spiritual values."

One reason why most people do not find the secret is they are unable to see in their mind's eye specifically what they desire. I myself have personally struggled with the visualization process. I have learned to use affirmations to compensate for my lack of visualization. I repeat over and over, "I am a success, I am a success, I am a success. I am a winner, I am a winner, I am a winner."

Affirmations are the key to building faith. The secret of faith is described as follows: "Faith is a state of mind which you may develop at will, after you have mastered the thirteen principles, because it is a state of mind in which develops voluntarily, through application and the uses of these principles. *Repetition of affirmation of orders to your subconscious mind is the only known method of voluntary development of the emotion of faith.*" Repetition is the operative word. This is a major secret.

Autosuggestion is the key to access the subconscious mind, and this is one of the most powerful secrets. It is the mastery of learning to use your mind in the most efficient way. Put simply, we can consciously connect with the subconscious mind by giving ourselves suggestions. For example, as you make a conscious effort to see the secrets, it is suggested that you use all the five senses. I see the secrets, I feel the secrets, I taste the secrets, I hear the secrets, and I smell the secrets.

The art of meditation is one avenue to eventually reach the subconscious, but that technique of autosuggestion can have immediate effect on the subconscious. The whole book *Think and Grow Rich* should be used as your guide to autosuggestion. The "secret within the secret" is to continuously work on your mastery of the principles of success. This is a lifelong commitment.

The use of the subconscious mind is one of my favorite secrets. I have been fascinated with the complexity of this powerful apparatus. "There is plenty of evidence to support the belief that the subconscious mind is the connecting link between the finite mind of man and Infinite Intelligence," wrote Dr. Hill. "It is the intermediary through which one may draw upon the forces of Infinite Intelligence at will."

The final principle and the greatest secret of the book is how to develop the Sixth Sense. Truly it is a secret to access the sixth sense, and few men and women have achieved this dream. "The sixth sense defies description!" said Dr. Hill. "It cannot be described to a person who has not mastered the other principles of this philosophy, because such a person has no knowledge, and no experience with which the sixth sense may be compared. Understanding the sixth sense comes only by meditation through mind development *from within*. . . . This principle is the apex of the philosophy. It can be assimilated, understood, and applied only by mastering the other twelve principles."

What do you think, has your scotoma been removed? Do you see the secrets in front of your nose? Are the secrets more obvious now? Are the secrets more transparent? They are to me.

To return to the beginning, the last paragraph of chapter one states: "Principles That Can Change Your Destiny." For the principles to work, you have to change your habits and practice and live each of the principles on a daily basis. I hope you will pick up *Think and Grow Rich* with renewed interest and begin to apply the secrets every day.

About Fred Wikkeling

Fred Wikkeling is an International Motivational & Inspirational Speaker from the San Francisco Bay Area. Fred is a Certified Instructor for the Napoleon Hill Foundation and a Certified Instructor for Personality Insights, the premier company that administers the D.I.S.C. Personality Profile assessment. For your next event, contact Fred at discpeople@ gmail.com. Visit www.discpeople.com for more information.

Through some strange and powerful principle of "mental chemistry" which she has never divulged, Nature wraps up in the impulse of strong desire "that something" which recognizes no such word as impossible, and accepts no such reality as failure.

—NAPOLEON HILL

22

My Blinders Were on Tight!

by Christopher Lake
TEMPE, ARIZONA

I admit it: I didn't find the secret in *Think and Grow Rich* the first time I read it. Or the second. Maybe not even the third. I suspect part of the reason was I was trying too hard. I took Dr. Hill's words as a personal challenge:

If you are ready to put it to use, you will recognize this secret at least once in every chapter. I wish I might feel privileged to tell you how you will know if you are ready, but that would deprive you of much of the benefit you will receive when you make the discovery in your own way.

Having rarely failed in an intellectual pursuit (differential equations being a notable exception), and holding a degree in English literature, perhaps I was smug and overconfident about finding the book's message. Surely I could see the secret immediately. Add to that a dose of skepticism—just "think" and grow rich, how preposterous—and the blinders were on tight.

I didn't get much from my first reading of *Think and Grow Rich*, but I recall thinking it was full of pseudoscience and often strayed into irrelevant religious matters. I certainly didn't see the secret in every chapter, and I was irritated that I hadn't solved the puzzle. That was about five years ago.

Today I think I know the secret and I'm learning to apply it. I see parts of my life I'm sure I would not have without working to understand the Science of Success. It almost seems like cheating to tell the secret, but to be honest, just knowing the secret, hearing the sentence defining it, is meaningless. It's what you do with the secret that matters.

Most likely my fellow contributors have already spilled the beans: the secret is that your mind is an untapped power for creating the life you want. You really can think and grow rich; in fact, you can't possibly grow rich without thinking. That's what Dr. Hill's interviews with hundreds of successful men proved. The common denominator in all success is learning to control the power of the mind.

For me, the most powerful of the 17 principles is applied faith. I used to consider faith to be useless, even silly; like television, an "opiate of the masses." Growing up in an agnostic home—nonreligious, not anti-religious—meant I had no basis for understanding spirituality. I saw the word *faith* and immediately got an image of God (white beard and all—I did know Michelangelo). It was only after I began to study Dr. Hill's works that I realized that faith encompasses a much larger part of life than I had interpreted from childhood.

Simply opening up to the concept of faith was a fundamental shift in my thinking. I had to actually *stop* thinking and let go some of what I believed I knew before I could get a grip on my life. Once I started to learn about faith, I began to let spiritual matters come to mind for serious consideration, thoughts I immediately would have dismissed before. Even though faith is not solely a matter of church and religion, I found that attending Catholic mass with my wife made me feel . . . good. Maybe there was something to this faith thing after all.

In retrospect, I believe I was really looking for a deeper meaning in my life, and allowing faith to affect me was a crucial step toward that goal. But recognizing and accepting the power of faith is only half the principle: faith must be *applied* or it means nothing.

Applied faith sums up the entire science of success for me, because in that phrase is both the powerful idea, "thoughts are things," and the nemesis for most people, taking action. Using a positive mental attitude and living with faith that all things are possible has meant I can act with conviction that I'll succeed. (However, I will not try differential equations again just to prove my point.) I've always liked the saying, "It's easy to know what to do, but hard to do what you know." Once you've started to study the principles of success, doing what you know becomes easier and—best of all—a lot more fun.

I find it ironic that struggling to understand the secret of *Think and Grow Rich* was above all a failure to read and comprehend the title itself. It's right there in plain sight for anyone to read. I'm grateful that I found the secret, but even more grateful to learn the importance of applying it. I wish you great success in your practice of Dr. Hill's philosophy.

About Christopher Lake

Christopher Lake is a writer and direct marketing consultant and serves as webmaster for the Napoleon Hill Foundation. A certified instructor with the Foundation, he is an avid proponent of Dr. Hill's philosophy and attributes much of his own success to learning the 17 principles. He lives and works in Tempe, Arizona, and can be contacted through www.cmlstudios.com.

Truly, "thoughts are things," and powerful things at that, when they are mixed with definiteness of purpose, persistence, and a burning desire for their translation into riches, or other material objects.

—NAPOLEON HILL

23

What Is The Secret?

by John Stutte
ATLANTA, GEORGIA

What is the secret in the *Think and Grow Rich* that Napoleon Hill refers to and is supposedly said to be on every page of the book? It presumably is the famous Carnegie secret and what it is exactly, I believe, has always been described best in words chosen by Napoleon Hill himself. In fact, the very essence of the secret can be found in Hill's famous and most quintessential quotation: "What the mind can conceive and believe, it can achieve."

Numerous references to the power of thought are given in *Think and Grow Rich*. "Thoughts are things," "Definiteness of purpose is the starting place for all riches" and "We become what we think about" for example are all statements from the book making definitive declarations claiming without equivocation that our thoughts influence our lives and our life circumstances. They are designed to further the cultivation of will-power and positive thinking. But by themselves, these concepts do not embody the Carnegie secret. They only speak to a part of it. Hill as much as tells us this at the end of his preface:

As a final word of preparation, before you begin the first chapter, may I offer one brief suggestion which may provide a clue by which the Carnegie secret may be recognized? It is this—ALL ACHIEVEMENT, ALL EARNED RICHES, HAVE THEIR BEGINNING IN AN IDEA! If you are ready for the secret, you already possess one half of it, therefore, you will readily recognize the other half the moment it reaches your mind.

Hill's quotation in the opening paragraph does something in particular that is very special for us. It breaks the secret down into the two halves and it does so concisely and poetically. The key concepts are in the rhymes: Conceive, Believe, Achieve. You almost don't need the rest. The other words are a sort of filler to support a fabulous structure that already sits on a strong foundation. And each concept appears in the appropriate chronological order. Conceive first! Then Believe in it and you will Achieve it! To Conceive and to Believe are the essential components needed for achievement and the attainment of any desired outcome.

Dr. Hill wrote many things during his lifetime which articulate and re-articulate this simple, but very powerful and often elusive idea. He authored several books, including the classic, *Think and Grow Rich*, and the tomes Hill thought to be his true tour-de-force, *Law of Success*. Through the various iterations, the philosophy developed fully in *Law of Success* incorporating 17 different principles. For *Think and Grow Rich*, Dr. Hill pared them down to just 13 "steps": Desire, Faith, Autosuggestion, Specialized Knowledge, Imagination, Organized Planning, Decision, Persistence, Power of the Master Mind, Sex Transmutation, the Subconscious Mind, the Brain and the Sixth Sense. But the secret always comes down to this two-part elixir, which is at its heart. The first two principles in *Think and Grow Rich* are: Desire—corresponding to "conceive" and Faith— corresponding to "believe." The remaining principles are tools designed to help us connect the dots and carry out the pursuit of success. A Burning Desire when fueled by the power of emotions such as Faith becomes the master key to riches. Page by page, we are reminded of the two pillars of the philosophy—sometimes subtly—sometimes blatantly. Here are some examples from the chapter on Faith:

I believe in the power of DESIRE backed by FAITH, because I have seen this power lift men . . .

FAITH is the head chemist of the mind. When FAITH is blended with the vibration of thought, the subconscious mind instantly picks up the vibration, translates it into its spiritual equivalent, and transmits it to Infinite Intelligence, as in the case of prayer.

The emotions of FAITH, LOVE, and SEX are the most powerful of all the major positive emotions. When the three are blended, they have the effect of "coloring" the vibration of thought in such a way that it instantly reaches the subconscious mind, where it is changed into its spiritual equivalent, the only form that induces a response from Infinite Intelligence.

Love and faith are psychic; related to the spiritual side of man. Sex is purely biological, and related only to the physical. The mixing, or blending, of these three emotions has the effect of opening a direct line of communication between the finite, thinking mind of man, and Infinite Intelligence.

Many consider Hill's work to be an extension of the New Thought Movement, a spiritual movement which developed in the United States during the late 19th century and emphasizes metaphysical beliefs. It consists of a loosely allied group of religious denominations, secular membership organizations, authors, philosophers, and individuals who share a set of metaphysical beliefs concerning the effects of positive thinking, the law of attraction, healing, life force, creative visualization, and personal power. It promotes the idea that "Infinite Intelligence" or "God" is ubiquitous. One could make the case that Hill is purveying the Carnegie secret as a method to reach, have access to and communicate directly with a Higher Power, or, in other words, a way to pray effectively.

To "Conceive" is illustrated in several ways throughout the book and is called by many names, such as "visualization" and "desire." Hill writes over and over that the starting point of all achievement is desire, and most of the time he adds the word "*burning*," thus making it into a "Burning Desire." The mixing of Desire with Faith transfixes it into Burning Desire. Faith, or belief is the second half of the Carnegie secret and it is what differentiates a Burning Desire from a mere wish.

The remaining steps take us through a masterful development and support of the philosophy built upon the secret that is the mixing of Desire and Faith, i.e. Conceiving and Believing. Most of these steps lean more toward bolstering a particular half of the secret or the other. For example, the third step, Autosuggestion develops and supports Faith. Alternatively, these other steps lay out necessary action that inevitably stems from a Burning Desire and that are needed to yield the goal or Achievement, which will bring us full circle.

In the chapter on Specialized Knowledge, Dr. Hill tells us there are two kinds of knowledge: general and specialized. General knowledge being interesting, but little use in the accumulation of money, he shows a way to organize, and intelligently direct certain knowledge through practical plans of action, to the definite end of accumulating money. He tells us that knowledge becomes power only when, and if, it is organized into definite plans of action, and directed to a definite end.

Hill describes Imagination, the next step, as the literal workshop of the mind where all plans created by mankind are fashioned. This supports and bolsters Desire, and this is clearly stated in the chapter:

The impulse, the DESIRE, is given shape, form, and ACTION through the aid of the imaginative faculty of the mind.

It has been said that man can create anything which he can imagine . . .

MAN'S ONLY LIMITATION, within reason, LIES IN HIS DEVELOPMENT AND USE OF HIS IMAGINATION.

Hill describes two forms of Imagination for us:
SYNTHETIC IMAGINATION: Through this faculty, one may arrange old concepts, ideas, or plans into new combinations. This faculty creates nothing. It merely works with the material of experience, education, and observation with which it is fed. It is the faculty used most by the inventor, with the exception of the "genius" who draws upon the creative imagination, when he cannot solve his problem through synthetic imagination.

CREATIVE IMAGINATION: Through the faculty of creative imagination, the finite mind of man has direct communication with Infinite Intelligence. It is the faculty through which "hunches" and "inspirations" are received. It is by this faculty that all basic, or new ideas are handed over to man.

Synthetic Imagination to me has always equated to an earthly application of the imaginative faculty, while Creative Imagination has always seemed more ethereal and hints again at the idea of connecting with Infinite Intelligence.

Organized Planning helps us form a definite, practical plan, or plans, through which the transformation of the "thought" to a "thing" may be made. This chapter begins to flesh out the notion of a later step, the Master Mind, which is the powerful method of enlisting the minds, bodies and spirits of other persons in an alliance to achieve a mutually desired end or purpose.

The next chapter lays out the Decision step and here we are told that the LACK of it is a major cause of failure. Procrastination is described as the opposite of decision, and is to be defeated as a common enemy. Along with beginning to admonish us about pitfalls which can cause failure, Hill examines the importance of habit, and we are encouraged to develop the habit of making prompt decisions and to begin putting into ACTION the principles being described. As he does throughout the book, Dr. Hill cites in this chapter one of the many famous persons he interviewed along the way as he developed the philosophy of success. This time, it's Henry Ford. Hill shares with us that Ford's most outstanding quality was his habit of reaching decisions quickly and definitely, and changing them slowly, if at all.

Persistence, the next step, we are told is an essential factor in the procedure of transmuting Desire into its monetary equivalent. We are also told that the basis of persistence is the power of will and that will-power and desire, when properly combined, make an irresistible pair. Again we explore the idea of synthesizing desire with emotions and powers of the mind and yielding something more powerful than the sum of the parts.

The fire metaphor, or the notion of a "Burning Desire" is repeated in the development of this chapter on persistence. The quality of persistence and its relationship to the character of man is likened to what carbon is to steel and as we read on, the fire metaphor continues:

The author is checking you up at this point, because lack of persistence is one of the major causes of failure. Moreover, experience with thousands of people has proved that lack of persistence is a weakness common to the majority of men. It is a weakness which may be overcome by effort. The ease with which lack of persistence may be conquered will depend entirely upon the INTENSITY OF ONE'S DESIRE.

The starting point of all achievement is DESIRE. Keep this constantly in mind. Weak desires bring weak results, just as a small amount of fire makes a small amount of heat. If you find yourself lacking in persistence, this weakness may be remedied by building a stronger fire under your desires.

In the next chapter, the step on the power of the Master Mind principle is laid out in detail, and Dr. Hill stresses harmonious cooperation with others. He goes on to explore the phenomenon of "power" in life and in business. This chapter tells us what power is, how to attain it and how to handle it properly once it's attained. Hill reminds us:

No individual may have great power without availing himself of the "Master Mind."

Sex Transmutation, which Earl Nightingale labeled "Enthusiasm," is the next step and simply put, it is "the changing, or transferring of one element, or form of energy, into another." The emotion of sex brings into being an extraordinarily heightened state of mind. Hill's view is that within this step lies the means of transforming mediocrity into genius. Sex Transmutation is simple and easily explained. It means the switching of the mind from thoughts of physical expression, to thoughts of some other nature. Again the image of a "Burning Desire" is conjured, although its treatment here is careful, respectful and sometimes subtle.

The next two steps are the Subconscious Mind and the Brain. Both of these chapters delve into the logistics and science of thought and brain electromagnetic chemistry. Hill tells us how to control what is allowed into the mind in order to attain any desired outcome. In these chapters, we see both halves of the secret again:

You may VOLUNTARILY plant in your subconscious mind any plan, thought, or purpose which you desire to translate into its physical or monetary equivalent. The subconscious acts first on the dominating desires which have been mixed with emotional feeling, such as faith.

And again we see a reference to Infinite Intelligence:
THE SUBCONSCIOUS MIND WORKS DAY
AND NIGHT. Through a method of procedure,
unknown to man, the subconscious mind draws upon
the forces of Infinite Intelligence for the power with
which it voluntarily transmutes one's desires into their
physical equivalent, making use, always of the most
practical media by which this end may be accomplished.

Through the medium of the something Hill calls "ether,"
and in a fashion similar to that employed by radio broadcast-
ing technology, Hill states that:
... every human brain is capable of picking up vibrations
of thought which are being released by other brains.

In connection with the statement in the preceding
paragraph, he compares and considers the description
of the Creative Imagination, as outlined in the chapter on the Imagination step. He describes the Creative
Imagination as the "receiving set" of the brain, which
receives thoughts, released by the brains of others. It is
the agency of communication between one's conscious,
or reasoning mind, and the four sources from which
one may receive thought stimuli.

When stimulated, or "stepped up" to a high rate of
vibration, the mind becomes more receptive to the
vibration of thought which reaches it through the ether
from outside sources. This "stepping up" process takes
place through the positive emotions, or the negative
emotions. Through the emotions, the vibrations of
thought may be increased.

As we can see in these paragraphs, all the steps and all the concepts begin coming together to work in tandem focused by intense desire and propelled by the channeling of energy from positive emotions.

The last step in the book, the Sixth Sense bridges both halves of the secret once again. This chapter delves even more deeply into the concept of Infinite Intelligence. Finally, after he's been through the 13 steps, Hill adds a chapter warning again of the danger presented by fear and its relationship to the causes of failure.

During his lifetime, Hill sought many times over and over to find opportunities to prove that Desire and Faith working together will most certainly germinate a thought into a reality. He attempted to prove that the secret works absolutely, even in seemingly futile circumstances. His second born son had a congenital defect rendering him "deaf for life." Hill was determined to make his son experience and possess some kind of hearing. He would not allow his son to be sent to schools for deaf children or to learn sign language, because he did not want him to accept the condition as his reality. Rather, he instilled in his son a Burning Desire to hear.

Some might argue that these measures are too extreme by today's standards, but Dr. Hill explains his rationale in the book. In the chapter on the very first step, Desire, Hill spins the tale of his son for us and how he started out learning to adjust to a hearing world by clenching his teeth on a phonograph and feeling its vibrations. Blair Hill eventually achieved the same success as hearing persons were capable of in a generation where there were few resources for handicapped individuals. He actually became very productive and successful, establishing himself in New York as a salesman of hearing devices. While writing *Think and Grow Rich*,

Napoleon and his second wife were living with Blair in his apartment there.

Numerous people over the years have stated that even though they have read *Think and Grow Rich* over and over, they still can't unearth the secret Hill describes in its preface. They say they are unable to do so even if they try reading "between the lines." Hopefully this analysis of the book will be helpful in your next reading. And I do recommend another reading, and another and another. . . . My experience has been, and Dr. Hill has told us that it does work, that you have to persistently and consistently apply it over and over again in each endeavor. In other words, make it a habit. And bring to it the enthusiasm each time. And as simple as it is, it is seldom, if ever, easy. It's like physical exercise or any skill. It must be nurtured and honed. It is a technique which must be practiced over and over.

If the secret is still elusive or clear as mud, I apologize. Alas, I've done it, too. I've spent all these pages and words telling you again what is so elegantly crystallized and encapsulated in that marvelous quote from Dr. Hill. What the mind can conceive and believe, it can achieve.

About John Stutte

John Stutte was born and raised in Jefferson City, Missouri, where he was introduced to Napoleon Hill's work as an adolescent. After studying classical music and composition for a few years in college, he instead pursued a career in business. In 2002 he decided to return to his passion and has since produced the musicals "Nap!" in Chicago and "Eeek! A Mousical" off-Broadway in New York.

Every human being who reaches the age of understanding of the purpose of money wishes for it. Wishing will not bring riches. But desiring riches with a state of mind that becomes an obsession, then planning definite ways and means to acquire riches, and backing those plans with persistence which does not recognize failure, will bring riches.

—NAPOLEON HILL

AFTERWORD

The Lessons of Life Well Learned

by Don Green
WISE, VIRGINIA

Millions of people have read *Think and Grow Rich*, the best selling self-help book of all time, but most do not discover the secret promised to be hidden on every page. This observation is based on the tremendous number of inquiries the Napoleon Hill Foundation receives about this very issue.

The so-called "secret" to me is simply that ideas are used as the starting point of all fortunes. Our imagination puts us above all other animals in that man has conscious control of his own thoughts. Our imagination allows us to develop ideas. Ideas produce solutions to not only our needs but also our wants.

Why then have we not solved all our problems and live in Utopia? We see things not necessarily as they may actually be, but as we believe they appear. We get different messages due to different perspectives.

We can have 20/20 vision and still not see what is in front of us. Epictetus, a Greek philosopher, wrote almost two thousand years ago: "What concerns me is not the way things are, but rather the way people think things are." More recently, my colleague Judith Williamson wrote that by understanding how our minds work, we can improve circumstances that exist in our lives. The thoughts we receive allow us to make choices. The thoughts we have and act on will make huge differences in our lives.

There is an old saying that our habits make us. Our habits are made by repeating an act until it becomes second nature. It does not matter if it is a good habit. Every habit can have a very profound effect not only in our lives but also those we choose to associate with. For example, the habit of smoking becomes so involuntary that little thought is given to the act or the damage one is doing one's body. Surely a person who smokes in the presence of others or with small children in a car is not thinking. He or she is simply acting out a habit.

The so called secret in a book is whatever stirs our imagination and gets us to think. Do we want to just be entertained or do we wish to get ideas that we can use to make a better life for ourselves and for others? It is important to get our minds involved in order to lead a successful life. We can read books repeatedly and get different ideas even the tenth or twentieth time. It is not that the material has changed, but that we have. Our perspective has changed with experience.

What we read is important but "what we see" is much more important. It was Einstein who said, "Imagination is more important than knowledge." Let me give you an example from my banking and finance career.

When you drive by a vacant lot or a run-down building do you see a field overgrown with weeds, brush, and trash, or do you see a playground, a beautiful home, a bank, or a retail store? The difference between a plot of land worth $20,000 or $2,000,000 is creative vision. Of course financial rewards are only a small part of the reason we need to "think and grow rich," to see the secret is our imagination and realize we all have the capacity to get ideas, develop plans and then take the necessary action to see the ideas become reality. Without these action steps ideas are only dreams that might feel good but have little value for the future.

Psychologist Viktor Frankl, while captive in a German death camp, wondered what helped some prisoners to survive while most died. Frankl discovered that those that survived had a vision of the future, a mission to perform, some important work to do, while most others only saw a sure death ahead.

What people visualize with strong emotion tends to come true. Especially in hard times, seeing things differently is essential. Positive visions keep us going; we all need something to look forward to in our lives.

About Don Green

Don Green is the Executive Director of the Napoleon Hill Foundation and has taught Hill's PMA Science of Success course at the University of Virginia's College at Wise. Using his 45 years of banking, finance, and entrepreneurship experience, Green has led the Foundation's fundraising efforts since 2000. Green currently resides and works in Wise County, Virginia, Napoleon Hill's birthplace.